The Essential Dehydrator Cookbook for Beginners

Easy Homemade Recipes for Fruit, Jerky, Herbs and Vegetables to Be Prepared for the Incoming Crisis

Mark Turner

Copyright © 2022 - All rights reserved.

The content contained within this book may not be reproduced, duplicated,or transmitted without direct written permission from the author or the publisher.

Under no circumstances will any blame or legal responsibility be held against the publisher, or author, for any damages, reparation, or monetary loss due to the information contained within this book. Either directly or indirectly.

Legal Notice:

This book is copyright protected. This book is only for personal use. You cannot amend, distribute, sell, use, quote, or paraphrase any part,or the content within this book, without the consent of the author or publisher.

Disclaimer Notice:

Please note the information contained within this document is for educational and entertainment purposes only. All effort has been executed to present accurate, up-to-date, and reliable, complete information. No warranties of any kind are declared or implied. Readers acknowledge that theauthor is not engaging in the rendering of legal, financial, medical, orprofessional advice. The content within this book has been derived from various sources. Please consult a licensed professional before attempting anytechniques outlined in this book.

By reading this document, the reader agrees that under no circumstances is the author responsible for any losses, direct or indirect, which are incurred as a result of the use of the information contained within this document, including, but not limited to, — errors, omissions, or inaccuracies.

Table of Contents

Introduction

Reality television would want you to think that preppers are neurotic folks who race about accumulating food in underground bunkers while spewing conspiracy theories, but this is not the case. Most are regular folks living in the real world, just like you, who want to be ready to endure any crisis. Natural catastrophes like hurricanes and blizzards, as well as global crises like the collapse of the economy or war, are examples of the types of emergencies that fall under this category. What would you do, for that matter,if you just lost your job and did not have money for groceries? If you have some food for the lean weeks, your family won't have to worry about going hungry.

Having an adequate supply of food in advance is also a sensible move. When people hear about an impending disaster, such as a storm or a blizzard, they rush to the shop to clear off the shelves as quickly as possible. There is a chance that there will be nothing left at the shop by the time you get there if you cannot get there because you are working or for some other reason. If you purchase extra supplies in advance, you won't need to worry about any of those things since you'll already be ready for them.

Putting together an emergency food stockpile may be done through various methods, such as purchasing dry and canned goods, canning one's food, or drying items. Reading this book, you will learn how to properly dry different foods and store them for later use.

The food processing business utilizes one of the most time-honored unit activities known to man: food dehydration. It involves adding one or more energy sources to the food to increase its shelf life while simultaneously decreasing the amount of moisture the food contains. However, this definition does not include the process of removing water from food by mechanical pressing or the concentration of liquid meals.

The majority of the time, heat is provided to the meal by hot air, which also removes moisture from the food as it moves through the cooking process. A concurrent transfer of mass and heat must occur inside the food and the medium utilized to transport energy to the food to dehydrate food.

When techniques for dehydrating food are used that provide the food with energy via a medium other than hot air, air or another gas may be needed to remove moisture from the food. If you want to learn about different food dehydration methods and recipes, let's start reading this book now.

Chapter 1
A Guide To Dehydrating Food

Dehydrating food is one of the easiest ways to store it for longer. Drying is one of the most efficient and cost-effective methods to preserve your crop. It has been used for centuries to make food last longer without refrigeration. Itis also possible to reduce the weight of meals developed specifically for camping & backpacking, saving your back and budget.

The moisture level of your food is drastically reduced by drying it, which enables it to keep for a longer period while maintaining its excellent flavor. This is because drying your food will lower the amount of moisture it contains to between 5 to 20 percent. The bacteria responsible for food spoilage cannot thrive within that temperature range. The shelf life of your favorite foods may be significantly increased simply by eliminating anymoisture they contain.

Types of Food Dehydrating

There are a few approaches you may take to dehydrate the food you have, butsome of these approaches are more effective than others. This is because contemporary technologies have improved the rate of dehydration, minimizing the likelihood that your food will go bad. The following are someof the most widespread practices followed today.

Air Drying

Drying food in the air, much like drying food in the sun, is an age-old dehydration technique. The primary distinction is that air drying almost always occurs in the shade. This is because this strategy assists in preserving everything that requires shielding from the sun'srays. It is an effective method for handling fragile greens and herbs, particularly those set aside for use in culinary mixtures or herbal teas.

Oven drying

Food is dried using the oven at temperatures of about 140 degrees Fahrenheit using the oven drying method. Ovens are not the most effective dryers available on the market because of their relatively big size. However, if you want to dry things quickly, you won't need to purchase an additional appliance if you use one of them. Because you will need to keep the door propped open to allow the moisture to escape, they may also help warm up your home.

If you want to dry food in the oven, you need to be sure that it can get to alow enough temperature. Your food will be cooked instead of dried at temperatures above 140 degrees Fahrenheit.

Sun Drying

Approximately 12,000 years ago, humans began slicing fruit and drying it in the sunlight by hanging it on racks or lines. In locations with extended hours of intense sun, sun drying is a very efficient method. As a result of their location in the Mediterranean, ancient Romans often used dried figs and raisins in their diet.

However, the temperature has to be at least 86 degrees Fahrenheit, and the relative humidity needs to be at least 60 percent. Always remember that it takes many days for fruit to completely dry out. Put on a mesh screen and protect with a second screen to prevent flies and insects from landing on the food. Galvanized metal should be avoided.

After 3000 years have passed since the first time people dried figs in the sun, the technique used for solar dehydration is still very straightforward. There are currently hundreds of styles depending on two drying methods:

- Direct Method

- Indirect Method

Direct Method

Direct solar food dryers are easier and need less space than indirect dryers. The simplest approach to making a direct dryer is to design a frame of 2 × 2'scoated with screen, nylon, or plastic sheeting on all sides except one. Access to the food trays is provided via a second screen door on the remaining side.

Put one or more trays within the frame so the fruit may get direct sun heat while being shielded from pests and other animals. This approach works exceptionally well for plums, tomatoes and herbs. Be careful to check on the food regularly; if it hasn't completely dried out by the end of the day, bringthe trays inside the home.

There are a few downsides to utilizing a direct dryer:Foods might take longer to process.

- Foods may lose nutritional value owing to exposure to UV.

- Molds may grow if water is not removed fast enough.

Converting a solar oven into a dehydrator is one approach that may be taken to address these issues. Some solar ovens are now available with additional dehydration kits for sun drying food, designed to utilize the sun's power and decrease the time necessary for drying.

Indirect Method

These dryers often need greater square footage because of their two-chamber design, which consists of one chamber in which the food is put on trays or sheets and another chamber to absorb solar energy. This kind of clothes dryerhas a second chamber that circulates air that is heated by the sun.

The collecting box is a long wooden frame that is rather shallow and is positioned below and perpendicular to the drying chamber. The inside of the container is covered with sun absorbers, such as a window screen with a dark hue or layers of a metal lathe. Glass or plastic glazing may be used to construct the collection box's roof.

Whenever the dryer is in operation, the bottom of the box it is housed keeps its door open so that new air may be drawn in and passed over the absorbers. When air flows upward, it may heat up to a temperature that is up to 20 degrees higher than the temperature outdoors. The warm air rises and flows into the chamber that contains the food, and then it moves out of the room viavents on the ceiling, bringing with it the moisture that has been gathered fromthe fruits that have been processed.

An indirect dryer can process large quantities of food at once and provides more uniform temperatures, which enables the processing to be completed more quickly.

Solar Drying

The process of drying food using a dehydrator powered by the sun is called solar drying, an upgrade from sun drying. Solar drying does not need any power since it does not rely on heating elements or fans to move the air around. Solar dryers are meant to operate in the open air and often resemble little tabletop greenhouses.

Electric Dehydrating

Electric dehydrators are the result of combining time-tested drying methods with present-day technology to create something revolutionary. These little workhorses are outfitted with fans and heating components, allowing them to dry your food as rapidly and effectively as possible. This ensures that there is almost little risk of spoiling and that the finished product is delicious.

In addition, a temperature gauge and an adjustable dial are often includedwith the purchase of an electric dehydrator. Depending on the product you're processing, this might either hasten or slow the drying process. If your food dehydrator has a fan, you may want to think about utilizing it in your garage or some other location where the noise won't be an issue. This advice is especially useful to keep in mind if you want to use a food dehydrator during the warm summer months but don't want your living environment to get too hot.

Purchasing an electric dehydrator is smart if you anticipate doing muchdrying shortly. Because many goods, such as fruit, beans, and tomatoes, mature all at once, gardeners may get the most out of their crops even though processing them without much waste can be challenging.

Electric dehydrators often come equipped with fans that may be used to expedite the drying process. Certain models come complete with timers that may assist in maintaining a higher level of consistency throughout several batches. The vast majority of electric dehydrators come in a space-saving compact design, with a variable number of shelves to accommodate varied capacities.

When shopping for an electric food dehydrator, you should search for modelswith low wattage, a decent thermostat, and a fan with a low noise level. Placethe dehydrator in a room that has the capability of becoming warm since the heat generated by the device will be released into the surrounding space whileit operates.

Excalibur Dehydrator is an excellent appliance for drying:

- fish

- fruits

- nuts

- vegetablesgrains

- fruit

- leathersherbs

- jerky

Microwave Dehydrating

If you are a fan of cooking with a microwave and have a small quantity of food to dehydrate, you may want to think about utilizing the 'defrost' setting on your microwave to dry out fruits, herbs, and other foods. On average, it will take the fruits that have been microwaved anywhere from 20 to 40 minutes to dry completely; however, you should check on them often to ensure that they are not overcooked. It takes around two to three minutes for the microwave to finish cooking herbs.

What Can You Dehydrate?

Nearly any fresh food may be dehydrated; however certain products dry out and retain their texture and flavor better than others. Here are some favorites.

- Apples, pears, bananas, peaches, blueberries, apricots, and cherries are some fruits eaten as snacks, cut up and used in granola and trail mix, or dehydrated and used to make fruit leather.

- Ingredients for soups, stews, and meals that may be prepared while camping include onions, peas, carrots, beans, mushrooms and tomatoes.

- Grains such as barley, rice, quinoa, buckwheat and amaranth have been sprouted to keep their nutritional value and store them for use in flours, granolas, and baked goods.

- Meat & fish, such as ground beef, turkey, chicken, sliced meats, fresh fish; beef jerky may be added to meals while trekking or stored for use as components in soups and stews.

- After soaking or sprouting, nuts and seeds, such as almonds, walnuts, pecans, hazelnuts and macadamia, can be easily digested.

- Oregano, dill, lemon balm, basil, fennel, parsley, mint and hyssop are dried and used later in beverages, baked goods, and meals.

- Raw food diets may include the consumption of crackers, chips, bread, and granolas.

Dehydrating Tools

When preparing food for dehydration, the major objective is to obtain an equal thickness throughout the meal. Everything will lose its moisture at the same pace, giving you an outcome consistent across the board.

The spoiling of a whole batch may be caused by only one or two thicker pieces that don't dry out completely. Utilize the appropriate instrument for thetask at hand to maximize the quality of the end output.

Are you thinking of trying out dehydrating, but you're not sure what kinds of equipment you'll need to get started? Not nearly as many as you may believe! You'll find a list below to help you get started!

It's always exciting to see what new kitchen gadgets come out. They guarantee that their products will make your life easier in the kitchen, facilitate the preparation of meals, and provide joy in all aspects of your life.

However, there are instances when gadgets demand you to have additional storage space, as well as more things that you will need to clean. So, let's talkabout the necessary tools, the tools that would be nice to have, and the things that you probably don't need at all!

Apple Slicing Device

This tool for slicing apples has been a very long time and is very reliable. Thecast iron model is more than 20 years old and still going. When preparingfruit such as apples and pears, simultaneously slicing, peeling, and coring the fruit is a fruit preparation method that works like a charm.

Look for one that does not have any plastic components. The rubber suction cup on the bottom of the tool helps secure it to your countertop. Other variants come with a clamp; however, if your countertop isn't a conventional size, you may have some difficulty using it.

Sharp Knife

When it comes to dehydrating, having a decent knife that is also sharp willget you a long way. In addition to that, a fantastic cutting board is a must- have.

Dehydrators

The only thing you need is a dehydrator that has a temperature gauge. It doesn't need to be large and elaborate; it need not be made of stainless steelor even be an Excalibur.

Excalibur Dehydrator 3900 is recommended because it has a huge capacity, does not have any digital components, is quick, and has an excellent reputation in dehydrators.

In addition, Cosori is also a good option because of its low noise level and compact size. The Magic Mill is another choice with an additional shelf and the Nesco series. They are all excellent dehydrators that can be purchased at prices to suit any budget.

Enjoy your food while keeping in mind that the finest dehydrator is the one you already own and are using to store food away in the cupboard for later use.

Mats & Sheets

Because it is possible that your dehydrator does not come with these, you will need to either construct your own, find an alternative, or purchase onesdesigned to work with your specific machine. These are essential componentsfor the smooth operation of a dehydrator.

The use of parchment or baking paper may satisfy any need. It helps with fruits and prevents little bits from dropping through your trays simultaneously.

Fruit leather sheets come at various pricing points, ranging from affordable generic versions to more costly sheets that are brand-specific and made of silicone. Many of the more budget-friendly editions may be trimmed down to fit on almost any tray. Always look for the lipped silicone trays compatible with the Excalibur; they are fantastic.

Mesh sheets are similar to plastic canvas craft sheets, except they include a perforated pattern instead of being solid. It lets air pass through but catches tiny bits of the food dehydrated.

However, a wide variety of sheets and mats are available to purchase that are compatible with any dehydrator. Also, if you don't want to spend money on a lipped tray that you'll only use sometimes, you may use this tip to make a liquid tray out of standard leather sheets or baking/parchment paper insteadof purchasing one.

Food Processor

Slicing, dicing, and chopping items for soups, stews, and snacks may also be accomplished effectively with the assistance of a food processor or grater.

Airtight Containers

When storing dried meals, the container must be airtight; this need applies regardless of the container you want. A wide variety of choices are available; thus, choose the one that is most suitable for you.

Keep in mind that you want to choose a container with a capacity comparableto the quantity of food you will be storing.

If you are interested in learning more about the many types of containers and the reasons why they are important, there are some helpful ideas for selectingthe containers that are the best fit for you.

- Containers made of plastic, such as Prepware, Rubbermaid,

Tupperware, OXO, and other brands with excellent sealing.

- Jars for canning food are the most practical daily usage option. Commercial glass jars with tight-fitting lids, salsa jars, sauce jars, etc.

- Mylar bags, but not the sort that has zippers or windows since suchtypes of bags will let air through once some time has passed.

Although they are not required, the equipment listed below may make thetask of making or storing dried meals simpler for you.

Slicers or Choppers

If your knife skills aren't the best or you have problems with your fine motor skills, it's a good idea to have a tool that can assist you with the preparation work, such as peeling, slicing, cutting, dicing and other similar tasks.

A vegetable or onion chopper that slices, dices, swirls, and gathers the chopped ingredients are an excellent investment. It is an excellent instrument for preparing onions without worrying about shedding tears.

Always remembers that if you use a blade similar to this, you should safeguard your hand by wearing a protective cutting glove. This is true evenif you use the handguards with mandolines.

Grinders

In the kitchen, powders are what make everything go smoothly. They are an advantageous method for using your dehydrated products that add flavor without adding bulk, do not intrude on the picky palate, and can assist you in incorporating a significant amount of nutrients into your regular cooking, even if you despise the vegetables in question.

Vacuum Sealers

Vacuum sealing is a great technique to guarantee that your food will have a long shelf life. These sealers come in a variety of shapes and sizes.

How to Prepare Food for Dehydrating?

You can prepare foods for dehydrating by doing these things:

Peeling

Peeling anything before dehydrating it is not required. Removing the skins from fruits and vegetables is done primarily to remove any defects that may affect the flavor or presentation of the food. It's possible that removing the skins off non-organic fruit is another step you may take to reduce yourvulnerability to pesticides.

If you want the greatest results from dehydrating fruits and vegetables, slice them between a quarter and a half an inch thick. If at all feasible, slice the meat thinner.

If you wish to remove the skins of fruits such as peaches, apples, apricots, or tomatoes, you may do it by submerging the fruit in boiling water for up toone minute. After that, please put them in a bowl of cold water for another minute and a half or until the skins begin to wrinkly and peel back. Now, the skins may be removed quickly and effortlessly by hand.

Steaming

You can also steam veggies for two to five minutes to blanch them, even if they would ordinarily take longer to cook. Before the food is dried, doing thiswill help retain nutrients and avoid the loss of taste.

Blanching

Blanching refers to preheating the veggies, fruits, and meats you would later put in your dehydrator. It is common to practice boiling vegetables before drying them; this helps preserve the taste of the veggies, especially those that need a longer cooking time. To blanch veggies quickly and easily, lay themin the bottom of your steamer and heat some water in the bottom of the appliance. Steam the veggies for two to five minutes or until they are cooked.

Before drying some veggies, blanching them beforehand might help maintaintheir freshness and taste. The following are some of the most frequent veggies to blanch:

- Asparagus (3 to 5 minutes)

- Carrots (3 to 4 minutes)

- Broccoli (3 to 5 minutes)

- Corn (1 to 3 minutes)

- Cabbage (2 to 3 minutes)

- Peas (3 minutes)

- Green beans (4 to 5 minutes)

- Kale & Spinach (just until wilted)

Dipping for Color & Flavor

There is a good reason why dried fruit that has been processed professionally keeps its color and texture. It is often preserved by dipping it in preservatives. When applied to the fruit's surface, these preservatives assist in preservingthe fresh fruit's appearance and flavor. It is unnecessary to put your food through the process of drying in a preservative before doing so, but it is important to think about how to make your food last longer in storage. The following are effective choices for preventing light-colored fruits from turning darker over time.

Ascorbic Acid

- Put one tablespoon of pure ascorbic acid into one quart of water and stiruntil it's dissolved.

- The food should be sliced or diced before being added to the solution,and then it should rest for no more than an hour.

- Before putting the ingredients on the dehydrator trays, remove them, letthem drain, and give them a quick rinse.

- You should not have trouble locating ascorbic acid at your area'ssupermarkets or health food stores.

Citric Acid

- In a crystalline form, dissolve one tablespoon of citric acid in water.The same rules apply.

- The effectiveness of citric acid is just 1/8 that of ascorbic acid, and itwill make the flavor of your fruits sourer.

- You may get citric acid at the grocery shop or health food store in yourarea.

Fruit Juice

- Combine one cup of lemon juice with one quart of water and stir.

- After soaking for up to ten minutes, the fruit should be thoroughly drained.

- Like citric acid, fruit juice does not have the same effectiveness as ascorbic acid (approximately 1/6 as much), leaving a sour flavor on the fruit to which it is applied.

Sodium Bisulfite

- Dissolve one teaspoon of its powder in one quart of water to make sodium bisulfite.

- Soak the fruit in the solution for two minutes before removing it, allowing it to drain, and then washing it.

- Recycling this solution is not a good idea since it will lose some potency after use. Additionally, be wary of sulfite allergies since they are rather prevalent.

How to Dehydrate Fruits?

Pick high-quality fruit plucked at the peak of its ripeness for the greatest results when drying it. The sugar content of ripe fruit is at its highest point, which results in sweeter snacks. Be wary of anything overripe or damaged since they may turn completely black as they dry.

If you are going to keep the skins on the fruit, wash them first, then core orpit the fruit (if necessary) and slice it to an equal thickness. Place on trays for dehydration and dry at 135 to 145 Degrees F until pliable.

The time needed to dry fruits such as apples, peaches, bananas, and nectarines may vary from 6 to 16 hours. Figs, apricots, grapes, and pears might take approximately 20 to 36 hours to ripen fully. Within those periods, check the trays every two to three hours and rotate them if required.

Do not add fresh fruit to your dehydrator if you have already started processing an older batch; doing so will cause the fruit that has been partially dried to take in more moisture.

How to Dehydrate Veggies?

Vegetables need a shorter amount of time to dry than fruits, but they also go bad more rapidly. When preparing them, use caution, and make every effortto prevent the loss of their freshness before drying them. This includeskeeping them in the refrigerator or on produce-saving paper, preparing onlyas much as you can manage in a single load of dishes, and washing them in cold water.

Remove any rough sections of skin or stem and any bruises or scars using a pair of sharp scissors. Use a spiralizer or a food processor to slice the vegetables to an equal thickness. When it comes to drying time, shorter lengths are preferable to longer ones.

Dry at 125 Degrees F on trays that have not been overlapping in the dehydrator. Tomatoes and onions are the only exceptions; they should be dried at 145 Degrees F for the best results. The amount of time needed to dry the vegetable will vary from 4 to 10 hours according to the size of the pieces you cut.

If possible, you should avoid drying strong-smelling veggies simultaneously as vegetables with a more subtle odor. If these vegetables are included, other meals will take on the distinctive aroma of peppers, brussels sprouts, onions, and garlic.

How to Dehydrate Meat & Fish?

When drying food, choose only fresh, lean cuts of meat and fish that are low in fat since the fat will become rancid much more rapidly. Pork should not bedehydrated unless you are using ham that has been cut and cured.

When drying cooked meat, trim off any excess fat and chop the meat into about half an inch cubes. Spread out on trays, then dry at 145 Degrees F. The majority of cooked meats will need between six and twelve hours for complete drying. If oil rises to the surface during dehydration, pat it dry. Similarly, you may also dehydrate ground beef that has been cooked.

To prepare jerkies for snacks and camping excursions, the beef must be slicedinto thin strips that are consistent with one another. The next step is to refrigerate the meat for anywhere between six and twelve hours while it is brined or dry-cured using a salty "rub."

After the dried strips, wipe them off and dehydrate them at 160 degrees Fahrenheit. Reduce the temperature to 145 degrees Fahrenheit and wait until the strips crack when bent but do not break.

How to Dehydrate Seeds & Nuts?

When wet sunflower seeds are already delicious in their raw form, there is noneed to dehydrate nuts and seeds. People who have digestive troubles may find that soaking and drying nuts and seeds make them simpler to manage. This may be the case. This is due to the presence of enzyme inhibitors in raw nut products. Putting nuts and seeds in water overnight helps break down the inhibitors that prevent digestion, making them easier to digest.

Soaking nuts in a solution of salt and water for a whole night is the first step in dehydration (about 1 tablespoon sea salt to 4 cups of nuts covered in water). After draining, spread the mixture in a single layer on the dehydrator'strays. Dry in an oven set to 145 degrees for 12 to 24 hours. Cashews, pumpkin seeds, almonds, pecans, and walnuts are delicious when prepared using this technique.

How to Dehydrate Herbs?

Drying herbs is one of the simplest and fastest methods for preparing dishes. The amount of preparation required is minimal, and they may be stored for a long time without suffering any taste loss.

Gather your preferred herbs first thing in the morning, and do it as early inthe year as possible, ideally before the flowers blossom. When the sun is out and the weather is dry, the best time to collect seeds like coriander and celery is in the morning. To hang in theshade, snip into lengths of a single stem, collect into a bundle, and then hang.

Alternately, spread out in a single layer on dehydrator trays and dry attemperatures between 95 & 105 degrees Fahrenheit for two to four hours. When herbs have reached their last drying stage, they become brittle and maybe easily broken apart when handled.

Then hold individual branches of the herb over a sheet pan or a piece of beeswax cloth and brush your fingers down the length of the stems to removethe leaves. Collect and store in airtight jars.

Some edible herbs that are commonly grown and dried for cooking are:

- Rosemary

- Oregano

- Mint

- Thyme

- Sweet

- Marjoram

- Lovage

- French

- Tarragon

- Coriander

Herbs exposed to sunlight will lose their vibrant colors and decline in quality.

If you want to stop dust from accumulating on your herbs, you may protect the foliage by putting it in paper bags with holes. If your drying location is exposed to a lot of sunshine, this may help lessen the risk of UV damage. Keep in mind that the stems of your herbs will contract as they dry out. You may need to occasionally tighten the string or other materials so the herbs don't tumble down.

It is possible to successfully dry herbs on window screens laid horizontally orin a dehydrator set to a low temperature. This method is particularly usefulfor drying herbs prone to mold growth, such as mint, or for drying smaller sprigs and flowers that cannot be tied in a bundle. Ensure that there is no overlap in the distribution of the foliage on the flat surface by spreading it outequally.

When your herbs have reached maturity, you will notice that they havebecome brittle and are readily broken apart. After this point, you may separate the leaves from the remaining stems, crush them to the properconsistency, and store them in containers to enjoy the whole year.

Frequently Asked Questions

Here are answers to some common questions about dehydrating food:

How long will food that has been dehydrated stay fresh?

Although dried food has been found to remain edible for up to 10 years if it is properly prepared and kept, the optimal time to consume it is between four months and one year after purchase.

Does dehydrating food destroy or preserve any of its nutrients?

Dehydrating food may eliminate certain nutrients, but not much more than other food preservation techniques. Light and heat are the two main culprits in the decomposition of vitamins. That means preserving food by canning removes more nutrients than dehydrating it at a low temperature with low humidity.

By blanching portions of your veggies, you may reduce the quantity of thiamin and vitamins A and C lost from your vegetables.

Does the process of dehydrating food eliminate bacteria?

If you dry your fruits and veggies until their moisture levels are between 5 and 20 percent, you will eliminate the bacteria that causes food to rot. This is the only method that guarantees success. Suppose you are concerned aboutthe presence of germs on meat.

In that case, the USDA suggests heating raw meat to 160 Degrees F and then dehydrating the meat at a temperature of 145 Degrees F.

Is it possible to dry out food with an Instant Pot?

Sadly, the answer is no. Even though an Instant Pot is an excellent multi-tool that can be used for slow cooking, pressure cooking, and even producing yogurt, it cannot dehydrate anything since it contains too much moisture. Even with the cap off. Even. Have faith in what we say.

Does the process of dehydrating food make it more sugary?

Because sugar is concentrated throughout the drying process while water vapor is removed, dried fruit has an especially sweet flavor. Dried fruit has a higher total amount of sugar than fresh fruit, but the amount of sugar in each gram of dried fruit is lower than that of fresh fruit.

Does dehydrating food harm enzymes?

There are exceptions to this rule. The killing of enzymes results from subjecting food to higher temperatures during drying. Denser foods can resist greater temperatures without losing enzymes; however, most enzymes become inactive as temperatures climb over 140 to 158 degrees F. Denser foods can withstand higher temperatures without losing enzymes.

Can you dehydrate home-cooked food?

Yes, you can. You can even dehydrate cooked food, although some dehydrate finer than others. However, if you are dehydrating for camping, hiking, or long-term food stockpile, you may pre-make stews, soups, rice dishes, saucesand even desserts and then dehydrate them by spreading them on a non-stick sheet and setting them on dehydrator trays. Some cooked foods dry betterthan others.

When they have achieved a wet but crumbly consistency, remove the non- stick sheets and allow them to dry the rest of the way.

What is the best way to preserve dry food?

Store your food in clean and dry jars (home canning jars or mason jars are good options for this), or pack it into freezer containers or silicone bags with lids that fit tightly.

Chapter 2

How To Store Dehydrated Foods?

Have you ever considered learning how to keep goods after dehydrating? Here is a beginner's guide to everything you need, which, in reality, is not very much!

What Containers & Bags Should You Use?

When keeping goods that have been dried, it is necessary to use airtight containers. You have the following options to choose from:

Canning/ Mason Jars

Canning containers and mason jars provide the greatest degree of convenience and adaptability in their usage. They may be used in their natural state, provided they are stored in a jar that has a capacity comparable to that of the food being preserved. In other words, if you have a tiny bit of dried food, you shouldn't use a massive jar to store it.

Jars should be clean. A hot wash with soap and water is sufficient, but you may run them through the sanitizing cycle on your dishwasher or boil them ifyou wish the additional clean, dry, and free of knicks and cracks before beingfilled with food. The fact that canning jars may be used several times before being thrown away eliminates any potential for waste. They also can be vacuum sealed, which helps to increase the shelf life of the food.

You could have some luck getting your reusable canning lids to seal by using a brake bleeder, but since there is no safe, tried-and-true technique with guaranteed results, you should only use these lids for canning and ordinary dry storage.

Vacuum Sealing Bags

Although they are ideally suited for storing things destined for the freezer, vacuum bags can accommodate dried foods that are not pointed or pointy. Byenabling air to enter even the tiniest of puncture holes, sharp and pointed edges might ultimately pierce the plastic, destroying all of your hard work. These vacuum-seal bags made by a generic brand work just as well as those made by a name brand!

When used with items that have been dehydrated, it is recommended to first wrap the dried food in parchment paper before placing it into the vacuum sealbag to be sealed. This helps to safeguard the bags from being punctured.

Keep in mind that many dried foods are easily broken into little bits and that the process of vacuum sealing and storing them might cause them to be crushed and broken up further. When you go grocery shopping for the first time, get a bag far larger than you anticipate. You can make them last longer by opening, washing, and then cutting them down for reuse.

Mylar Bags

These bags are recommended to preserve dried foods and other items long- term. They can be vacuum-sealed easily if an O2 absorber is used, and they can also be vacuum-sealed if the version with the rough interior is used.Dried foods do not readily pierce them, but they are not rodent-proof; thus, you should store them in rodent-proof bigger canisters if necessary.

Do not use mylar bags with transparent windows or zipper tops when storing items for an extended period. Both choices let air get through, so your storagewill become ineffective after a certain time.

Airtight Containers

It doesn't matter what airtight container you choose, as long as you test it to ensure it is airtight. It is not airtight if you can press the sides and hear air escaping; this indicates that the seal is broken. Commercial glass jars with tight-fitting lids, Tupperware or other plastic containers with airtight seals, and lids with silicone inserts are also suitable options.

Zipper Bags

Although they are not suitable for keeping short-term or long-term items,they are suitable for storing lesser amounts, which may subsequently bestored in a bigger airtight container. Make sure to utilize the more substantial freezer versions, however.

Additionally, they are suitable for foods like fruit leathers that will be stored in the refrigerator for a few days, as well as jerky that will be stored in the freezer for a month or two.

Where to Store Dried Foods?

Places that are cold and dark are ideal for storing goods that have been dehydrated. The ability of food to be stored well may be compromised by several factors, including light, heat, oxygen, and moisture.

The ideal locations to keep your dehydrated meals are:A closet

- A bookshelf with a cover

- A cabinet

- A food-grade bucket

Tips for Storing Dried Foods?

Prioritize cleanliness; nothing more frustrating than removing dried fruitfrom your machine, placing it in storage and then discovering that it has developedmold two months later. If you dry it well, you shouldn't have anyproblems.

- Package the product in smaller amounts. Rather than attempting to keepit in a huge container that will be exposed to air every time you open it, consider using a smaller container for daily usage and a larger container for storing the surplus.

- The powder just as much as you need, dried goods have a longer shelf life while they are in their complete form as opposed to their powder form, so only powder as much as you require for the next month or two.

- Mark the jars clearly; dried herbs all have the same appearance, and some may have lost their distinctive aroma. When you have a lot of powders, they start to blend and seem the same. Please put the name of the food item and the date it was dried on each of your jars.

How Long Do Dehydrated Foods Last?

The shelf life of dried foods may range anywhere from one to two years if thefood is properly dehydrated, conditioned, and stored. On the other hand, in many instances, you should be able to get a few more years out of it.

Foods may be preserved for much longer periods if vacuum-sealed correctly. Most foods are still safe to consume after two years, even though theirtextures may start to change; in some foods quicker than other foods, tomatoes are an excellent example. Some consumers report that their meals retain their freshness and flavor even after being stored for up to five years!

If foods are correctly prepared, dried, conditioned & stored according to the NCHFP's safety criteria, then the following are true:

- Dehydrated foods have a shelf life of up to two years.\

- Powders for the next six to nine months

On the other hand, we know that dried foods may remain edible for at least five years in practice. However, certain items, like tomatoes, may lose their flavor, texture, and color sooner than others, so it is important to keep an eye out for these changes. Blanching is vital for drying out various foods for this reason and many others!

On the other hand, powders have a shorter shelf life than herbs and spices because a much greater proportion of the product's surface area has been subjected to processing and, as a result, has been exposed to light, heat, air, and moisture. Therefore, it is advisable to keep it in its complete form and powder it when needed.

O2 Absorbers Vs. Desiccant Packs

Both are optional components in the process of dehydrating food in ordinary life. You are not required to use a moisture absorber, even though doing so might be beneficial and provide you with some peace of mind. O2 absorbers are only really required if you do not possess the tools to vacuum seal the container and want to preserve the item for an extended time. However, ifyou employ either one of them properly, they both have the potential to makeyou feel less anxious. And please never use them in conjunction with one another.

Moisture absorbers, silica gel sachets and desiccant packs are different namesfor the same product. They are variants of the things that may be found in places such as shoe boxes, different packaging, vitamin bottles, and several other containers. But refrain from putting any of them in your diet. In most cases, they are unsafe for consumption or contain contaminants you do not want to find in your food. In most cases, a 2-gram moisture absorber is required for a jar up to a quart in capacity.

- Moisture absorbers have the following benefits:

- Help maintain dry fruits' moisture by removing extra air from the jar.

- Assist in regulating moisture levels in containers you are constantly moving in and out of.

- It can be reactivated by drying it in an oven preheated to 250 degreesfor two to three hours.

- They can be reused; this is the reason why they are deserving of one's financial consideration. They aren't that costly, to begin with, and you can use them more than once!

If you want to experiment, you may make your desiccant packets, or you can use a moisture absorber that you make yourself using the DIY option. Don't combine oxygen absorbers and moisture absorbers in the same container.

Because the O2 absorbers depend on the presence of moisture for theiroperation, using a desiccant pack is ineffective.

O2 absorbers are the devices that are used in the process of removing oxygen from a container. This does not affect helping to regulate moisture; all it does is eliminate oxygen from the air. They

are not designed to be used in opened and closed containers regularly. This is because the absorbers cannot be reused and are rendered ineffective when exposed to the elements. These containers are designed for long-term storage.

They assist in regulating oxygen levels in storage containers that cannot have a vacuum created inside of them, such as food-grade buckets, mylar bags, or big jars. Jars containing a lot of space and from which you want to guarantee that all of the oxygen has been eliminated might benefit from adding oxygen control measures.

A helpful hint to follow when shopping is to spend a little bit more and buy items in smaller quantities to help reduce the risk of exposure. When attempting to deal with them, you run a considerably lower danger of exposing all of them if you have many tiny bags of 5 each rather than one large bag of 100. This causes the price of the smaller bags to be somewhat higher.

Other Options

Utilizing a vacuum sealer is the most convenient and cost-effective alternative to acquiring and fumbling about with oxygen absorbers. Although it does not eliminate all of the oxygen in your jar, it does get rid of most of it, which is sufficient for the year or two that most dried items are suitable for.

Additionally, certain foods are heavy in fat that you do not want in an environment devoid of oxygen; this is why preserving tomatoes in oil is not a good idea because moisture plus bacteria plus oxygen equals botulism.

Chapter 3
Chips And Crackers

Dehydrated Corn Chips

Prep Time: 15 minutes | Cook Time: 30 minutes

Dehydration Time: 10 hours | Servings: 4

INGREDIENTS

- 2 tsp of salt

- 1/2 cup of flaxseed ground

- 1/4 cup of water

- 2 tbsp of apple cider vinegar

- 1 yellow bell pepper

- 4 cups of frozen corn

INSTRUCTIONS

1. To get a smooth mixture, use a food processor or blender to combine allingredients, excluding the flax or linseed.

2. After adding the flax, continue blending until it is completely incorporated.

3. After spreading the dough between two nonstick dehydrator sheets, cutthe mixture into the desired shape using a cookie cutter.

4. Dehydrate the ingredients at 115°F for 8-10 hours, flip them onto amesh tray and continue drying for 12 hours, or until they become crisp.

5. Keep a few months in a container that seals well to keep air out.

NUTRIENTS:

Kcal: 283, Fats: 10 g, Total Carbs: 47 g, Proteins: 28 g.

☆ ☆ ☆ ☆ ☆

Cinnamon Apple Chips

Prep Time: 15 minutes | Cook Time: 0 minutes

Dehydration Time: 12 hours | Servings: 4

INGREDIENTS

- 1 tbsp of ground cinnamon

- 1/4 cup of sugar

- 4 apples

INSTRUCTIONS

1. Apples need to be washed and cored.

2. Apples should be sliced into thin rounds with a mandoline or a sharpknife, and the thickness should be between 1/8 and 1/4 inches.

3. Cinnamon and sugar should be mixed in a separate basin.

4. Prepare apple slices for dehydration by arranging them in a single layeron mesh sheets for the dehydrator.

5. Sugar and cinnamon, mixed, should be sprinkled over the apple slices.

6. Dehydrate in an oven preheated to 135°F for 10-12 hours.

7. Let the temperature return to room temperature.

8. Keep in a location that is cool and dark with an airtight container.

NUTRIENTS:

Kcal: 167, Fats: 0.4 g, Total Carbs: 44.7 g, Proteins: 0.7 g.

☆ ☆ ☆ ☆ ☆

Pear Chips

Prep Time: 10 minutes | Cook Time: 1 hour

Dehydration Time: 10 hours | Servings: 10

INGREDIENTS

- 10 Pears

INSTRUCTIONS

1. Pears should be sliced with the skins still on, and you should discard thecore. Place the slices on the dehydrator trays in such a way that they donot touch one another.

2. Let the pears dry in an oven set to 130°F for 8-10 hours, or until they have a leathery texture and no wet patches.

3. Place in a container that is suitable for food storage.

NUTRIENTS:

Kcal: 101, Fats: 1 g, Total Carbs: 27 g, Proteins: 1 g.

☆ ☆ ☆ ☆ ☆

Mushroom Chips

Prep Time: 20 minutes | Cook Time: 30 minutes

Dehydration Time: 6-8 hours | Servings: 5-6

INGREDIENTS

- 1/2 tsp of powdered garlic

- 1/2 tsp of dried parsley

- 1/2 tsp of sea salt

- 1 tbsp of lemon juice

- 1 pound of mushrooms

INSTRUCTIONS

1. If you choose, you can cut the tips off the mushroom stems, but be sure to leave them intact. To cut mushrooms into slices approximately 1/8 ofan inch thick, you can use a grinder fitted with a slicing blade or aknife.

2. Slice the mushrooms and place them in a large basin. Add some lemon juice, sea salt, garlic powder, and chopped parsley on the top. You can avoid breaking up the mushrooms by using your hands to toss themixture to distribute the spice gently properly.

3. Put a dehydrator tray over the sink, and then remove approximately halfof the mushrooms that have been seasoned using a large spoon or just carefully scooping them out of the bowl. They should be spread out equally around the dehydrator tray and can touch one another, but they shouldn't be piled up because this prevents air distribution.

4. Proceed with the remaining half of the mushrooms in the same manner.

5. Dehydrate on high for 4-6 hours, or until the substance is dry and crisp.

6. Once it has cooled, it can be served or stored in an airtight container.

NUTRIENTS:

Kcal: 31, Fats: 2 g, Total Carbs: 7 g, Proteins: 3 g.

Potato Chips

Prep Time: 20 minutes | Cook Time: 10 minutes

Dehydration Time: 8 hours | Servings: 15

INGREDIENTS

- 5 cups of water
- 1 tsp of alum
- 1 tbsp of sea salt
- 5 pounds of potatoes

INSTRUCTIONS

1. Prepare the potatoes by slicing them very thinly using a mandolinslicer.

2. Bring the water, salt, and alum to a boil in a kettle.

3. Put the potato slices into a pot of water, bring them to a boil, and cookthem for five minutes.

4. Take them out of the water. Put them in a separate saucepan filled withcold water for a few minutes.

5. Drain the surplus water out of it.

6. Arrange them out in an even layer in a dehydrator, or do the same in theopen air.

7. Dehydrate for 6-7 hours until crisp or in direct sunlight for one to twodays.

8. Keep it in a jar that seals well and is airtight.

9. When you are ready to dine, fry the food in hot oil.

NUTRIENTS:

Kcal: 150, Fats: 10 g, Total Carbs: 15 g, Proteins: 2 g.

☆☆☆☆☆

Cucumber Chips

Prep Time: 10 minutes | Cook Time: 30 minutes

Dehydration Time: 4 hours | Servings: 6

INGREDIENTS

- 2 tsp of vinegar

- 1 tsp of salt

- 1 tbsp of olive oil

- 2 medium cucumbers

INSTRUCTIONS

1. Slice the cucumbers extremely thinly to maintain a uniform thickness while they dry. If you want the best possible results, slice everything on a mandolin if you have one. Use an extremely sharp knife if you cannot access a mandolin.

2. To eliminate as much moisture as possible from the cucumber slices, patthem dry with a paper towel. Put the cucumbers in a bowl that's big enough to hold them, then add the rest of the ingredients. To incorporateeverything, toss it together lightly yet completely.

3. For dehydrator: Arrange slices of cucumber on trays, and dry them at 135°F for 12 hours, or until they attain the appropriate level of crispiness.

4. When preparing for the oven, place the slices on a baking tray linedwith parchment paper. Dry them at 1750°F for 3-4 hours, checking on them once an hour to ensure they don't get burnt or brown around the edges. Flip them over when they reach the halfway point.

5. Before serving, the slices should be allowed to cool.

NUTRIENTS:

Kcal: 29, Fats: 2 g, Total Carbs: 1 g, Proteins: 1 g

Zucchini Chips

Prep Time: 15 minutes | Cook Time: 15 minutes

Dehydration Time: 8 hours | Servings: 4

INGREDIENTS

- 1/2 tsp of salt

- 1 tsp of grated garlic

- 2 tbsp of freshly ground thyme

- 2 tbsp of sesame seeds

- 2 tbsp of olive oil

- 3 Zucchini

INSTRUCTIONS

1. Scrub and pat dry the zucchini.

2. You can use a bread or meat cutting machine or do it by hand if you want the slices to be perfectly thin.

3. Put all of the zucchinis in a bowl and sprinkle them with olive oil,thyme that has been freshly ground, sesame seeds, garlic, and salt.

4. After thoroughly combining everything with care, spread it out on the plates of the dehydrator.

5. In my case, the highest setting on the dehydrator is 70°C. To ensure thatthe drying process is carried out evenly, rotate the

plates every two hours.

6. After it is finished, place it in the airtight container, or you can enjoy it.

NUTRIENTS:

Kcal: 137, Fats: 12 g, Total Carbs: 6 g, Proteins: 3 g.

☆ ☆ ☆ ☆ ☆

Crispy Bread Chips

Prep Time: 10 minutes | Cook Time: 10 minutes

Dehydration Time: 20 minutes | Servings: 3

INGREDIENTS

- 1 tbsp of olive oil
- 1/4 tsp salt
- 3 garlic cloves
- 1 tsp of parsley
- 2 bread rolls

INSTRUCTIONS

1. Slice each of the bread rolls into uniformly thin pieces. You might want to cut them in half a second time if they are exceptionally large.

2. Put the slices of bread in a single layer on a baking sheet covered with

3. parchment paper. The bread slices should not overlap one another.

4. Mix the garlic cloves that have been minced, the parsley, and

the salt inthe olive oil.

5. Spread the mixture on the bread slices using a paintbrush.

6. Toast the bread pieces in the oven for ten to fifteen minutes, or untilthey have a crisp texture and golden brown color.

7. Serve with spinach hummus, traditional hummus, or guacamole.

NUTRIENTS:

Kcal: 125, Fats: 5 g, Total Carbs: 15 g, Proteins: 2 g.

☆ ☆ ☆ ☆ ☆

Apple & Flax Cracker

Prep Time: 30 minutes | Cook Time: 1 hour

Dehydration Time: 8 hours | Servings: 15

INGREDIENTS

- 1 tbsp of lemon juice
- 1/2 tsp of ground cinnamon
- 1/2 cup of coconut butter
- 2 tbsp of coconut nectar
- 1/2 cup of butternut squash puree
- 1/2 cup of ground flax
- 1/2cup of water
- 5 apples

INSTRUCTIONS

1. Add apples, squash puree, coconut nectar, butter, cinnamon, and lemonjuice to a container.

2. Add water to it. Water helps make a smooth batter.

3. Add flax to the food processor and pulse until mixed.

4. Smooth the batter to 1 / 4 thickness on 3-4 parchment-lined dehydratortrays.

5. 12-hour dehydration at 118°F. Remove the parchment from the crackerbatter before dehydrating.

6. Dehydrate for 6-8 hours more, or until dry. Break or cut the crackersinto rectangles.

NUTRIENTS:

Kcal: 150, Fats: 1 g, Total Carbs: 10 g, Proteins: 6 g.

☆ ☆ ☆ ☆ ☆

Nuts & Seed Crackers

Prep Time: 30 minutes | Cook Time: 30 minutes

Dehydration Time: 10 minutes | Servings: 4

INGREDIENTS

- 1 teaspoon of sea salt

- 1/4 cup of golden flaxseed meal

- 1/2 cup of golden flax seeds

- 1/2 cup of pumpkin seeds

- 1/2 cup of chia seeds

- 1/2 cup of sunflower seeds

- 1 1/2 cups of water

- 1/2 cup of hazelnuts

- 1/2 cup of almonds

INSTRUCTIONS

1. Start preheating the oven. Position a rack, so it is directly in the centerof the oven. Preheat the oven to 175°C.

2. Prepare the nut material. Process the almonds, hazelnuts, and pumpkin seeds into a fine meal using a food processor fitted with a blade. You might also process the sunflower seeds. Mix if you don't like a lot of different textures in your food.

3. Place all of the nuts and seeds, as well as the sunflower seeds, psyllium,and salt, in a sizable bowl, and stir until everything is well distributed.

4. Repeat the mixing process after adding the water. Add surplus water if the mixture is too thick or if parts of the dry ingredients aren't entirely soaked.

5. Spread the mixture out on a surface. Roughly divide the mixture into two equal parts.

6. Place the first half of the mixture on a sheet of parchment paper, cover itwith one more sheet, and roll it out into a thin sheet.

7. If the mixture is rolled out and you find that it has any holes, simplytake a little piece of the mixture and use it to patch the hole.

8. Take off the top layer of parchment paper, then use the sharp point of a knife to score the mixture into any shapes you choose.

9. Bake. After transferring the mixture onto a large baking sheet with the bottom piece of parchment paper, bake for

approximately 30 minutes, turning the mixture over once halfway through the cooking process.

10. If you see that one side of the crackers has browned more than the other,you should flip the baking sheet so that the crackers will have the best opportunity of baking evenly. In most cases, I perform this step once, at the three-quarter mark of the baking period.

11. Cool. Place the baked "cracker" on a cooling rack and let it cool to roomtemperature. It should then break the cracker following the lines that have been scored.

12. Store. Store leftover crackers for up to one week in a jar that sealstightly and is kept at room temperature. Store in an airtight jar for one month for longer-term storage.

NUTRIENTS:

Kcal: 57, Fats: 4 g, Total Carbs: 4 g, Proteins: 2 g.

☆ ☆ ☆ ☆ ☆

Crackers Bread

Prep Time: 5 minutes | Cook Time: 30 minutes

Dehydration Time: 8 hours | Servings: 28

INGREDIENTS

- 1-5 cups of water

- 1/4 cup of white chia seeds

- 1/3 cup of dark flax seeds

- 1/2 cup of golden flax seeds

- 1 cup of sesame seeds

INSTRUCTIONS

1. Get all of the seeds ready.

2. Put all the seeds in a single, larger basin and combine them with thatbowl.

3. Put approximately 1 / 4 cup of the mixture into a coffee grinder. Turneverything into a powder, then put it back into the original bowl.

4. Blend the powdered seeds into the whole seeds completely with yourspatula, and then add the water.

5. Continue stirring the mixture until all of the water has been absorbed.Allow it to sit for anywhere between 5-10 minutes.

6. When you notice the mixture has thickened, spread it out on a bakingpan lined with parchment paper or on a tray for a dehydrator.

7. A silicone spatula is ideal for spreading the mixture as evenly and thinlyas possible.

8. Start the procedure by loading all the trays into the dehydrator andturning it on.

9. You may dehydrate the mixture in the oven at 70° by spreading it out on a baking dish wrapped in parchment paper and then drying it in theoven.

NUTRIENTS:

Kcal: 43, Fats: 4 g, Total Carbs: 0 g, Proteins: 2 g.

Carrot Crackers

Prep Time: 18 minutes

Dehydration Time: 10 hours | Servings: 8/10

INGREDIENTS

- 2 cups carrot pulp
- 1 cup almonds, soaked overnight and drained
- 2 tbsps ground flax seed
- 1 tbsp chia seeds
- 1 tbsp dried onion
- 1 tbsp coconut aminos
- 1/2 teaspoon smoked paprika
- 2 cups water

INSTRUCTIONS

1. In a food processor, add the almonds and pulse until crumbly.
2. Add the rest of the ingredients and pulse until everything is fullycombined.
3. Spread a thin layer of the dough in the food dehydrator and dry for twohours at 120 F.
4. To create the crackers, score the dough.
5. Dry for eight hours at 115°F.

NUTRIENTS:

Kcal: 120, Fats: 7.5 g, Total Carbs: 11 g, Proteins: 4 g.

Dehydrated Seed Crackers

Prep Time: 1 hour

Dehydration Time: 9 hours | Servings: 10

INGREDIENTS

- 1 cup water
- 3/4 cup flax seeds
- 1/4 cup chia seeds
- 1 1/3 cup sunflower seeds
- 1 tbsp Italian seasoning
- 1 tbsp pumpkin seeds
- 1/4 cup hemp seeds
- Salt and pepper

INSTRUCTIONS

1. Soak the flax seeds and chia seeds in water for 1 hour.
2. Drain and transfer to a bowl.
3. Add the rest of the ingredients and mix well.
4. Dry at 115 F for 90 minutes.
5. Then flip and break into smaller pieces and dry at 105°F for another 8hours.

NUTRIENTS:

Kcal: 180, Fats: 13.5 g, Total Carbs: 10.5 g, Proteins: 4.5 g.

★ ★ ★ ★ ★

Dehydrated Sweet Potato Chips

Prep Time: 15 minutes | Cook Time: 0 minutes

Dehydration Time: 4 hours | Servings: 2

INGREDIENTS

- 2 teaspoon onion powder

- 2 sweet potatoes, scrubbed and sliced.

- Salt

INSTRUCTIONS

1. Put the sweet potatoes in a food dehydrator and dry at 155°F for 2hours.

2. Flip and dry for another 2 hours.

3. Season with salt and onion powder.

NUTRIENTS:

Kcal: 190, Fats: 3.4 g, Total Carbs: 19.7 g, Proteins: 3.7 g.

☆ ☆ ☆ ☆ ☆

Banana Chips

Prep Time: 15 minutes | Cook Time: 0 minutes

Dehydration Time: 12 hours | Servings: 5

INGREDIENTS

- 5 bananas, sliced thinly

- 1 teaspoon of lemon juice

INSTRUCTIONS

1. Season with the lemon juice the bananas and add to the food

dehydrator.

2. Dry for 12 hours at 135°F

NUTRIENTS:

Kcal: 71, Fats: 4.2 g, Total Carbs: 27 g, Proteins: 2.1 g.

☆ ☆ ☆ ☆ ☆

Banana Cracker with Peanut Butter

Prep Time: 4 hours and 15 minutes | Cook Time: 0 minutes

Dehydration Time: 6 hours | Servings: 10

INGREDIENTS

- 3 bananas sliced

- 3 cups graham cracker crumbs

- 1 cup ground peanuts

- 1/2 cup peanut butter

- 1/2 teaspoon cinnamon powder

INSTRUCTIONS

1. In a bowl, combine the bananas, peanut butter, and remaining ingredients.

2. Roll the dough to form a long rectangle, cut it and refrigerating it forfour hours in wax paper.

3. Add the slices to the food dehydrator and dry at 150°F for 6 hours.

NUTRIENTS:

Kcal: 180, Fats: 13 g, Total Carbs: 11 g, Proteins: 5 g.

☆ ☆ ☆ ☆ ☆

Chapter 4
Side Dishes

Dried Zucchini

Prep Time: 45 minutes | Cook Time: 5 minutes

Dehydration Time: 50 minutes | Servings: 4

INGREDIENTS

- 1 tsp of sesame oil
- 1 tsp of salt
- 1 tsp of garlic
- 1/2 stalk scallion
- 1 cup of dried zucchini slices

INSTRUCTIONS

1. To rehydrate the dried zucchini slices, soak them in filtered clean water for 30 minutes. After draining the water, give the zucchini a lightsqueeze to remove any excess moisture. The zucchini slices ought to be tender and malleable at this point.

2. Reduce the rehydrated zucchini slices to bite-sized pieces with a knife.

3. You should heat a skillet over medium-high heat and add the rehydratedzucchini pieces, garlic, and scallion to the pan. Salt the food after it has been sautéed for around 3-4 minutes. The chewiness should not be overpowering, though. If you need the zucchini to have a softer texture, add some water, then continue to sauté the vegetables for an additional 1-2 minutes.

4. It can be stored in the refrigerator for three days if sealed in an airtight container.

NUTRIENTS:

Kcal: 16, Fats: 1 g, Total Carbs: 1 g, Proteins: 1 g.

Mashed Potatoes

Prep Time: 20 minutes | Cook Time: 1 hour

Dehydration Time: 8 hours | Servings: 12

INGREDIENTS

- 1 pounds of potatoes

INSTRUCTIONS

1. Scrub potatoes. Peeled chunks won't rehydrate as well. It should cut each potato into four pieces. Boil cold water over potatoes. Simmer potatoes for 20 minutes.

2. Reserve potato juice.

3. Start mashing potatoes with reserved liquid. Blend until smooth, addingliquid as required. Make your mashed potatoes runnier than usual to get a smooth leather that turns powder.

4. You can season the mash now or wait till the end.

5. Spread mash on Paraflex or parchment-lined dehydrator trays. Spread evenly.

6. 8-10 hours at 135°F will make mashed potatoes dry and brittle. When the dried mash breaks crisply off the liner, they're done. Not just bendable, but crispy and breakable.

7. Cool completely before storing.

8. Use a coffee grinder, blender, or food processor to powder your leather. Finer processing speeds up and smoother rehydration.

9. Cool, dry, dark storage is best. Best quality within a year, but safe for much longer. Vacuum seal for long-term storage.

NUTRIENTS:

Kcal: 27, Fats: 0 g, Total Carbs: 9.7 g, Proteins: 2.3 g.

☆ ☆ ☆ ☆ ☆

Dehydrated Marshmallows

Prep Time: 5 minutes | Cook Time: 1 hour

Dehydration Time: 2 hours | Servings: 6

INGREDIENTS

- 1 bag of miniature marshmallows

INSTRUCTIONS

1. Arrange the marshmallows in a layer on the trays of the food dehydrator. If you give each one a little space around it, the marshmallows won't clump together into one massive mass as they puffup.

2. In our dehydrator, we used fruit leather trays so the fruit would adhereto the bottomless, but your dehydrator may be different. If your dehydrator has temperature control, set it to 160°F. Don't worry about itif you don't have it; turn it on. Dehydrate yourself for 2-3 hours.

3. When the marshmallows have lost some puffiness and are dry on the outside, you should begin testing them. Test them repeatedly until you are certain that they are totally dry.

4. Marshmallows should be allowed to cool before being stored in an airtight jar in the pantry.

NUTRIENTS:

Kcal: 120, Fats: 0 g, Total Carbs: 29 g, Proteins: 0 g.

☆ ☆ ☆ ☆ ☆

Dehydrated Cauliflower Popcorn

Prep Time: 10 minutes | Cook Time: 12 hours

Dehydration Time: 12 hours | Servings: 2

INGREDIENTS

- 1 tsp of smoked cayenne

- 1/2 tsp of ground cumin

- 1 tbsp paprika

- 4 tbsp hot sauce

- 3 tbsp coconut oil

- 1 head of cauliflower

INSTRUCTIONS

1. After giving the cauliflower florets a quick rinse, slice them into pieces that are just a little larger than popcorn. Put it in a bowl with the remaining ingredients and toss to combine. Ensure that all of the seasonings are perfectly distributed over them. If you feel it's necessary,add a few more drops of spicy sauce to the mixture.

2. Dehydrate the mixture for eight to twelve hours at a temperature of 130°F, or until it is completely dry. Place the mixture on a couple of dehydrator trays. You can still consume them when they are not dried out, but doing so will produce a more chewy texture. If you let the "popcorn" dry out completely, it will have a crunchier texture.

3. Put them in airtight baggies and store them in a cold, dry area. Enjoy

NUTRIENTS:

Kcal: 264, Fats: 22 g, Total Carbs: 15 g, Proteins: 7 g.

☆ ☆ ☆ ☆ ☆

Potato Wedges

Prep Time: 10 minutes | Cook Time: 5 minutes

Dehydration Time: 1 hour | Servings: 6

INGREDIENTS

- 3-4 tbsp of avocado oil

- 1 tsp of salt

- 1 tsp of garlic powder

- 1/2 tsp of dried red pepper

- 1/2 tsp of dried parsley

- 1/2 tsp of dried oregano

- 6-8 potatoes

INSTRUCTIONS

1. After washing potatoes, cut them lengthwise into quarters, then cut eachin half.

2. After bringing a medium saucepan of water to a boil, add the uncookedpotato wedges to the pot.

3. You should parboil the potato wedges for eight to ten minutes beforebeing drained.

4. While the potatoes are boiling, put the oil and seasonings in a smallbowl and set them aside.

5. Get the oven up to temperature, 425°F.

6. Apply the seasoned oil to both sides of the partially boiled potatowedges, then arrange them on a baking sheet or an air

fryer tray.

7. Put the dish in the oven and bake it for about 45-55 minutes, until thepotato wedges are browned and crisp.

8. While the potatoes are baking, combine all of the ingredients for the dipping sauce in a ramekin or other similarly sized container.

9. Once the potatoes have reached the desired doneness, remove themfrom the pan and serve them immediately with the dipping sauce.

NUTRIENTS:

Kcal: 47, Fats: 0 g, Total Carbs: 17.9 g, Proteins: 1.2 g.

☆ ☆ ☆ ☆ ☆

Baguette Toast

Prep Time: 10 minutes | Cook Time: 30 minutes

Dehydration Time: 1 hour | Servings: 40

INGREDIENTS

- 1 tablespoon of Kosher salt

- 1 teaspoon of black pepper

- 1 cup of extra-virgin olive oil

- 1 baguette

INSTRUCTIONS

1. Set the temperature of the oven up to 350°. Place bread slices on a baking sheet to form a single layer.

2. Ladle some olive oil on each side of the meat. Sprinkle salt and pepper on both sides of the meat.

3. Toast the bread slices for approximately 12 minutes, during which time you should rotate the baking sheet from front to back and flip the slices halfway through the baking process.

4. And this will ensure that the toasts are evenly browned and crispy throughout.

5. Toasts can be stored overnight in zipper-lock bags at room temperature as long as they are covered.

NUTRIENTS:

Kcal: 62, Fats: 2 g, Total Carbs: 8 g, Proteins: 2 g.

Chapter 5
Vegetable Recipes

Risotto With Vegetables

Prep Time: 5 minutes | Cook Time: 30 minutes

Dehydrating Time: 6 hours | Servings: 2

INGREDIENTS

- 1 tsp of salt

- 1 tbsp of oil

- 1 tbsp of parmesan cheese

- 1 onion

- 2 cups of broth

- 2 tbsp of olive oil

- 1/2 cup of white wine

- 1 cup of rice

- 1/4 cup of peas

- 6-8 mushrooms

- 1 zucchini

INSTRUCTIONS

1. Add onion and salt to a pot and cook for 6 minutes. Sauté rice for 1-2 minutes, till translucent. Stir the wine until it evaporates. Add the broth and boil, stirring constantly and adding a half cup of water as required. Let the risotto cool in the pot.

2. Slice zucchini and mushrooms as the risotto cools.

3. Dehydrate zucchini, mushrooms, and peas, ensuring they don't overlap. Mesh or solid tray liners or parchment paper can line additional dehydrator trays. Evenly spread risotto on the tray.

4. Dehydrate vegetables and risotto for 4-8 hours at 135°F. Store in an airtight jar until camping.

NUTRIENTS:

Kcal: 684, Fats: 23 g, Total Carbs: 95 g, Proteins: 12 g.

☆ ☆ ☆ ☆ ☆

Strawberry Twizzlers

Prep Time: 15 minutes | Cook Time: 30 minutes

Dehydration Time: 24 hours | Servings: 4

INGREDIENTS

- 1 pound of strawberries

- 1 tsp of strawberry extract

- 2 cups of dates

INSTRUCTIONS

1. Be sure to thoroughly clean the beetroots and then roughly cut them intomanageable pieces for the juicer's feeding tube. Chop some beetroots and then put them in a blender with a little water. After that, place the pulp in a nut bag or another type of mesh bag and press the bag to extract the juice. Although it needs quite a bit of effort, it is not impossible.

2. With the "S" blade attached to the processor, process the beet juice, strawberry extract and date paste until it is thoroughly combined.

3. Spoon the batter in a bag with a plain star tip pre-installed. My diameterof mine was approximately 0.6 millimeters.

4. Initially starting at one edge and working your way to the

other, pipe thebatter onto a Teflex sheet. Applying constant pressure will help you generate a straight line.

5. Dehydrate at 115°F for 24 hours. Wait until everything has cooled downbefore putting it in an airtight container.

NUTRIENTS:

Kcal: 150, Fats: 1 g, Total Carbs: 35 g, Proteins: 1 g.

☆ ☆ ☆ ☆ ☆

Dehydrated Pumpkin Leather

Prep Time: 5 minutes | Cook Time: 15 minutes

Dehydration Time: 24 hours | Servings: 8

INGREDIENTS

- 1/2 tsp of ground allspice

- 1/2 tsp of ground nutmeg

- 1 tsp of ground cinnamon

- 1/4 cup of honey

- 1 cup of coconut milk

- 1/4 cup of shredded coconut

- 2 cups of apple sauce

- 2 cups of pumpkin puree

INSTRUCTIONS

1. Combine all the ingredients, but don't add the cranberries or the raisins.

2. Either drop by the tablespoon to make cookies or spread the mixture onfruit leather sheets thoroughly oiled and placed in

a dehydrator.

3. You can sprinkle dried cranberries or raisins on top of the pumpkinmixture if you'd like.

4. Dry for 8-24 hours at a temperature of around 135°F.

5. Squares or slices can be cut from the meat. Roll up.

NUTRIENTS

Kcal: 178, Fats: 9.1 g, Total Carbs: 26.3 g, Proteins: 1.7 g.

Vegetable Yellow Curry

Prep Time: 20 minutes | Cook Time: 20 minutes

Dehydration Time: 8 hours | Servings: 2

INGREDIENTS

- 1 tbsp of Thai yellow curry paste
- 4 tbsp f coconut milk powder
- 2 cups of frozen vegetable mix
- 2 pounds of basmati rice

INSTRUCTIONS

1. Cook the rice, drain and then allow cooling gently.

2. Separately, distribute the rice, vegetables, and curry paste across thedehydrator trays.

3. Cover each tray with a nonstick sheet or parchment paper.

4. 4–8 hours of drying time at 135°F/57°C.

5. Place the dried food in a bag that can seal with a zip lock. After addingthe coconut milk powder, close the jar.

NUTRIENTS:

Kcal: 445, Fats: 17.2 g, Total Carbs: 61.1 g, Proteins: 7.6 g.

Teriyaki Mushroom Jerky

Prep Time: 1 hour | Cook Time: 12 hours

Dehydration Time: 20 hours 15 minutes | Servings: 4

INGREDIENTS

- 1 garlic clove

- 1/2 inch ginger

- 1 tbsp of brown sugar

- 1 1/2 tsp of sesame oil

- 1 tsp of sriracha

- 1/4 cup of soy sauce

- 2 tbsp of rice vinegar

- 2 Mushroom caps

INSTRUCTIONS

1. Add all of the ingredients to a container.

2. Cut the mushrooms into pieces that are approximately 1/3 thick.

3. Marinate for around 8 hours in the tamari mixture, giving it a shake every so often to ensure an even coating.

4. Note that the mushrooms will exude some of their liquid into the marinade while it sits, so you will see that the volume of

the marinade has increased as it has had more time to absorb the liquid.

5. Dehydrate the mushroom slices at 125°F for about 12 hours. Place the mushroom slices on a dehydrator tray.

NUTRIENTS:

Kcal: 90, Fats: 2 g, Total Carbs: 7 g, Proteins: 1 g.

☆ ☆ ☆ ☆ ☆

Dehydrated Bell Peppers

Prep Time: 20 minutes | Cook Time: 15 minutes

Dehydrating Time: 18 hours | Servings: 20

INGREDIENTS

- 1 garlic clove
- 1/2 inch ginger
- 2 tbsp of brown sugar
- 1 1/2 tsp of sesame oil
- 1 tsp of sriracha
- 1/4 cup of soy sauce
- 3 tbsp of rice vinegar
- 20 bell peppers

INSTRUCTIONS

1. Deseed the peppers, and split them into pieces of a size that is pretty consistent.

2. Place the pepper pieces in a single layer on a tray intended for use in a dehydrator. Dehydrate the peppers by placing the tray

in your dehydrator.

3. Continue doing so until all the peppers have been included in the dish. After the trays have been completely inserted, you should place the cover on the dehydrator.

4. Dehydrate the peppers by heating them to 125°F for 12 to 24 hours.

5. If you are going to use them for long-term food storage, it is very important to check that they are fully dry and do not have any softnessto them in any way, shape, or form.

6. Keep the dried peppers in a jar made of mason glass.

NUTRIENTS:

Kcal: 23, Fats: 3 g, Total Carbs: 4 g, Proteins: 1 g.

Dehydrated Asparagus

Prep Time: 8 minutes | Cook Time: 0 minutes

Dehydrating Time: 6 hours | Servings: 4

INGREDIENTS

- 2 cups asparagus trimmed and sliced

- Salt

- Garlic powder

INSTRUCTIONS

1. Put the asparagus in the food dehydrator.

2. Dry at 130°F for 6 hours.

3. Season with salt or garlic powder

NUTRIENTS:

Kcal: 430, Fats: 43 g, Total Carbs: 20.5 g, Proteins: 5.2 g.

☆ ☆ ☆ ☆ ☆

Cauliflower Popcorn

Prep Time: 15 minutes | Cook Time: 0 minutes

Dehydration Time: 8 hours | Servings: 2

INGREDIENTS

- 2 cups cauliflower florets

- 1 tbsp paprika

- 1/2 teaspoon ground cumin

- 1 tbsp coconut oil

- 1 teaspoon smokedcayenne

- 1 tbsp hot sauce

INSTRUCTIONS

1. Put the cauliflower florets in coconut oil and hot sauce.

2. Mix well and add smoked cayenne, cumin and paprika

3. Put the cauliflower in the food dehydrator and dry for 8 hours at 130°F

NUTRIENTS:

Kcal: 10, Fats: 0 g, Total Carbs: 3 g, Proteins: 0.1 g.

☆ ☆ ☆ ☆ ☆

Dehydrated Beets

Prep Time: 15 minutes | Cook Time: 0 minutes

Dehydration Time: 12 hours | Servings: 6

INGREDIENTS

- 2 tbsp olive oil

- 4 beets sliced thinly

- 1/2 cup water

- 1/2 cup vinegar

- Salt

INSTRUCTIONS

1. In a bowl combine all the ingredients and marinate for 10 minutes.

2. Put the beet slices in the food dehydrator and dry for 12 hours at 135°F.

NUTRIENTS:

Kcal: 78, Fats: 4.1 g, Total Carbs: 26.7 g, Proteins: 1.8 g.

Dried Tomatoes

Prep Time: 18 minutes

Dehydration Time: 8 hours | Servings: 4

INGREDIENTS

- 4 tomatoes sliced into quarters

- Salt

INSTRUCTIONS

1. Season the tomatoes with salt.

2. Add the tomatoes to the food dehydrator.

3. Dry for 8 hours at 135 F.

NUTRIENTS:

Kcal: 250, Fats: 7 g, Total Carbs: 43 g, Proteins: 4.1 g.

Smoky Collard Green Chips

Prep Time: 20 minutes | Cook Time: 0 minutes

Dehydration Time: 6 hours | Servings: 4

INGREDIENTS

- 3 tbsp olive oil

- 1/2 tsp smoked paprika

- 1/4 tsp pepper

- 1/4 tsp salt

- 1 bunch collard greens

INSTRUCTIONS

1. In a bowl, put all the ingredients and mix well.

2. Place collard green in the food dehydrator and dry for 4 hours at 140°F.

NUTRIENTS:

Kcal: 15, Fats: 0.2 g, Total Carbs: 3.1 g, Proteins: 1 g.

Smoked Sweet Potato Chips

Prep Time: 10 minutes | Cook Time: 5 minutes

Dehydration Time: 6 hours | Servings: 4

INGREDIENTS

- 1/2 tsp of sea salt

- 3 sweet potatoes sliced thinly

- 2 tsp olive oil

- 2 tsp smoked paprika

INSTRUCTIONS

1. Put the potatoes in a pot of boiling water for 5 minutes.

2. Transfer the potatoes in a bowl of ice water.

3. Dry the potatoes and season them with the remaining ingredients.

4. Put potatoes in the food dehydrator and dry for 6 hours at 135°F.

NUTRIENTS:

Kcal: 35, Fats: 0.5 g, Total Carbs: 7.8 g, Proteins: 1 g.

Dried Marinated Eggplant

Prep Time: 2 hours | Cook Time: 0 minutes

Dehydration Time: 12 hours | Servings: 4

INGREDIENTS

- 1 egg plant

- Salt and pepper to taste

- 1/4 cup olive oil

- 1/2 tsp Sriracha sauce

- 1 tbsp maple sauce

- 1 tbsp balsamic vinegar

INSTRUCTIONS

1   Slice the eggplants and season with all the ingredients.

2   Put in the fridge for 2 hours.

3   Dehydrate the eggplant slices at 115°F for about 12 hours. Place theeggplant slices on a dehydrator tray.

NUTRIENTS:

Kcal: 19, Fats: 0.2 g, Total Carbs: 4.7 g, Proteins: 0.1 g.

☆ ☆ ☆ ☆ ☆

Dehydrated Spinach Balls

Prep Time: 20 minutes | Cook Time: 0 minutes

Dehydrating Time: 5 hours | Servings: 4

INGREDIENTS

- 4 cups blanched spinach

- Pepper

- 1/4 tsp nutmeg

- 5 tbsp olive oil

- 3 cloves of garlic

- 1/2 cup dehydrated onion flakes

INSTRUCTIONS

1   Combine all ingredients and whisk several times until well-combinedand pasty consistency.

2   Form bite-sized balls of spinach, and place them in the dehydrator anddehydrate at 120°F for 5 hours.

NUTRIENTS:

Kcal: 123, Fats: 13 g, Total Carbs: 9.4 g, Proteins: 4.1 g.

Dehydrated Sweet Kale Chips

Prep Time: 15 minutes | Cook Time: 0 minutes

Dehydration Time: 6 hours | Servings: 4

INGREDIENTS

- 1 bunch curly kale that has been cleaned, the stems cut off, and theleaves roughly ripped

- 1/3 cup water

- 1/2 cup pine nuts

- 1/2 tbsp cinnamon

- 1/4 cup white sugar

- 1/8 cup apple cider vinegar

INSTRUCTIONS

1. Combine cinnamon, sugar, and pine nuts in a food processor.

2. Blend vinegar and water and add slowly to food processor.

3. Pour the mixture over the kale, then toss to coat.

4. Place at 140°F for 4 hours on dehydrating trays.

NUTRIENTS:

Kcal: 109, Fats: 8 g, Total Carbs: 9.5 g, Proteins: 1.8 g.

☆ ☆ ☆ ☆ ☆

Dehydrated Vegan Broccoli Chips

Prep Time: 10 minutes | Cook Time: 15 minutes

Dehydration Time: 12 hours | Servings: 8

INGREDIENTS

- 4 heads broccoli, washed and cut into bite size florets
- 1/2 tsp red pepper flakes
- 1 tsp curry powder
- 1/2 cup cashews, soaked for 1 hour and drained
- 3 tbsp nutritional yeast

INSTRUCTIONS

1. Blend all the ingredients, except for broccoli, in a food processor.
2. Add water to achieve a smooth texture.
3. In a bowl, pour dressing and add broccoli.
4. Mix well and place florets onto dehydrator sheets and dehydrate al110°F for 12 hours.

NUTRIENTS:

Kcal: 108, Fats: 6.9 g, Total Carbs: 8.3 g, Proteins: 5.7 g.

☆ ☆ ☆ ☆ ☆

Chapter 6
Meat & Fish Recipes

Beef Jerky In A Dehydrator

Prep Time: 1 hour | Cook Time: 6 hours

Dehydration Time: 7 hours | Servings: 5

INGREDIENTS

- 1 tsp of salt

- 2 tsp of brown sugar

- 1 tsp of red pepper flakes

- 1 tsp of black pepper

- 2 tsp of liquid smoke

- 1/4 cup of soy sauce

- 1/4 cup of Worcestershire sauce

- 1 Lean Beef

INSTRUCTIONS

1 Choose a beef cut that is low in fat. Remove the fat cap as well as any other visibly excess fat. Once trimmed, you should place the meat in thefreezer for 1-2 hours or until it is half frozen. You will have more consistent slices when you cut the beef this way.

2 Put the ingredients for the marinade into a plastic bag or container witha lid that can seal tightly, and then combine them thoroughly.

3 Cut meat from the refrigerator and slice it across the grain into 14-inch strips. This will make it easier to chew. Jerky will have more chewiness if it is cut with the grain.

4 After adding the sliced meat to the marinade: Give it a good shake to ensure that each slice is coated uniformly.

5   Place it in the refrigerator. Let it marinade for anywhere between 6-24 hours.

6   Shake the container or bag two or three times during the marinating process.

7   Once the slices have been marinated, pat them dry using paper towels toremove any excess marinade.

8   Put the strips on the dehydrator's drying racks, leaving plenty of room between each rack for the air to circulate freely.

9   Dry for 3 hours at a temperature of 165°F, enabling the internal temperature to rise to 160°F before lowering it to 145°F. Check themeat after it has been drying for four hours, and continue drying the jerky until it bends and splits but does not break in two.

10 Before keeping jerky, it should be let cool down for many hours.

NUTRIENTS:

Kcal: 70, Fats: 4 g, Total Carbs: 5 g, Proteins: 21 g.

Dehydrated Ground Beef Jerky

Prep Time: 5 minutes | Cook Time: 1 hour

Dehydration Time: 8 hours | Servings: 4

INGREDIENTS

- 1 tsp of salt

- 1 tbsp of sugar

- 1 tbsp of lemon zest

- 1tsp of ground black pepper

- 1/8 tsp of cayenne pepper

- 2 tsp of sweet paprika

- 2 tbsp of grated onion

- 2 tbsp of lemon juice

- 1 tbsp of olive oil

- 1 tbsp of Worcestershire sauce

- 1 tbsp of soy sauce

- 1 clove garlic

- 1/2 tsp of liquid smoke

- 1 pound of ground beef

INSTRUCTIONS

1   Let the ground beef be chilled until you are ready to use it.

2   In a bowl, mix all spices with beef. Let the rest of the ingredients for 15minutes for the flavors to get mixed.

3   Add the ground beef and combine well. Put it in the refrigerator for 1hour.

4   Spread a sheet of waxed or parchment paper on a surface. Scoop 1/4 of the jerky mixture onto it. Put the second sheet on top and roll it out to a thickness of 1/4 inch.

5   Put a dehydrator tray on top of the jerky.

6   Dehydrate at 155°F for 4 to 8 hours. Keep a check after 4 hours. You want the jerky fully dried. Don't be worried if you're not 100 percent sure you've correctly identified that consistency; the next step helps ensure food safety.

7   When the jerky is dried but still chewy, transfer it to baking

trays andset the temperature at 275°F for 10 minutes. Jerky is too runny for a meat thermometer, ensuring it is fully cooked.

8   Cut it into strips. After it is perfectly cool, store it in airtight containers at room temperature.

NUTRIENTS:

Kcal: 367, Fats: 23 g, Total Carbs: 7 g, Proteins: 32 g.

☆ ☆ ☆ ☆ ☆

Dehydrated Salmon Jerky

Prep Time: 30 minutes | Cook Time: 1 hour

Dehydration Time: 7 hours 30 minutes | Servings: 12

INGREDIENTS

- 1 tsp of lemon juice
- 4 tbsp of soy sauce
- 1/4 tsp of garlic
- 1 tsp of liquid smoke
- 2 tsp of black pepper
- 1 tsp of molasses
- 4 pounds of Salmon

INSTRUCTIONS

1   Fresh Salmon often has bones that can be dehydrated. Gently peel out the bones. Peel the salmon skin with a sharp knife, starting at one end. Remove only the salmon skin to preserve the flesh.

2   Place Salmon on parchment paper and freeze until frozen solid. A sharpknife can easily cut frozen fish into salmon strips.

3   Crosswise, slice the fish 0.5 cm thick. Keep the strips the same thickness for even drying. Each strip should be 2 cm.

4   Blend the marinade ingredients. Pour marinade over fish in a bag.Refrigerate for 3.5 hours.

5   Strain fish and marinade through a sieve to dehydrate. Pickled fish tearseasily.

6   Salmon slices should be blotted and arranged in rows on the dehydrator surface. Avoid overlapping salmon strips. Dehydrate for 3-4 hours at 145°F.

NUTRIENTS:

Kcal: 236, Fats: 16.8 g, Total Carbs: 0 g, Proteins: 22 g.

☆ ☆ ☆ ☆ ☆

Dehydrated Pemmican

Prep Time: 45 minutes | Cook Time: 1 hour

Dehydration Time: 24 hours | Servings: 6-8

INGREDIENTS

- 3-4 tsp of dried berries

- 1/2 pound of meat fat

- 2 pounds of meat

INSTRUCTIONS

1. Thinly slice the meat, 14 to 1/3 inch.

2. Remove any fat from meat and dry it over a fire, in the sun, in

a dehydrator, or in an oven. The traditional drying method involves hanging strips on thin branches or racks above a fire for nearly 12hours.

3. Once dry, crush the meat. Using contemporary conveniences, you may mill it into a fine powder. This labor-intensive phase can be donemanually. Adding berries requires drying and pulverizing.

4. Render the fat separately until it stops foaming.

5. Strain out solids.

6. Slowly add rendered fat to the powdered meat in a bowl or casserole dish. The powder will absorb fat as you pour, so ensure it's uniformly distributed and not too runny.

7. Once the fat is absorbed, let the mixture cool and harden for a fewhours. Storage options include squares or balls.

NUTRIENTS:

Kcal: 11, Fats: 1 g, Total Carbs: 3 g, Proteins: 1 g.

☆ ☆ ☆ ☆ ☆

Pastrami Jerky

Prep Time: 24 hours

Dehydration Time: 6 hours | Servings: 6

INGREDIENTS

- 3 pounds lean beef

- 1 tbsp mustard seeds

- 1/2 cup soy sauce

- 2 tbsp coriander seeds

- 1/2 tsp cayenne pepper

- 1/4 cup brown sugar

- 1 tbsp lemon juice

- 2 tbsp coarse pepper seeds

- 1/2 cup Worcestershire sauce

INSTRUCTIONS

1. Each beef slice should be divided into 1/4-inch-thick strips.

2. Combine all the ingredient, except seeds, and pour over sliced meat.

3. Put in the fridge overnight.

4. Remove the meat from refrigerator and let come to room temperature.

5. Sprinkle the meat with the seeds an put in the food dehydrator.

6. Dehydrate at 150°F for 6 hours.

NUTRIENTS:

Kcal: 60, Fats: 1.4 g, Total Carbs: 5 g, Proteins: 6 g.

☆ ☆ ☆ ☆ ☆

Smoked Turkey

Prep Time: 15 minutes | Cook Time: 0 minutes

Dehydration Time: 16 hours | Servings: 4

INGREDIENTS

- 1 pound of lean turkey

- 1/2 tbsp paprika

- 1/4 cup brown sugar

- 2 tbsp liquid smoke

- 3/4 cup soy sauce

- 1 tbsp smoked paprika

INSTRUCTIONS

1. Slice turkey into 1/4 inch thick strips.

2. Combine all ingredients and pour the entire mixture over the turkeystips. Refrigerate the turkey for 4-6 hours covered.

3. Slices of turkey should be dried at 155° F for 12 to 16 hours.

NUTRIENTS:

Kcal: 75, Fats: 1.4 g, Total Carbs: 11 g, Proteins: 5.8 g.

Garlic Beef Jerky

Prep Time: 16 minutes | Cook Time: 0 minutes

Dehydration Time: 8 hours | Servings: 6

INGREDIENTS

- 1 tbsp. Worcestershire sauce

- 2 tbsp. Ketchup

- 2 tsp. Red hot sauce

- 1 tsp. Fresh lime juice

- 2 pounds thinly sliced beef

- 1 can of coke

- 7 cloves crushed garlic

- 1/2 cup soy sauce

INSTRUCTIONS

1. In a big basin, mix the marinade ingredients. Put the meat in a ziplockbag and cover it with the marinade.

2. Meat should be marinated for 4 to 8 hours.

3. Place meat in a single layer on dehydrator sheets.

4. Dehydrate for 6 to 8 hours at 155°F.

NUTRIENTS:

Kcal: 56, Fats: 1.8 g, Total Carbs: 1.8 g, Proteins: 7.2 g.

Beef Jerky with Mustard and BalsamicVinegar

Prep Time: 12 hours | Cook Time: 0 minutes

Dehydration Time: 6 hours | Servings: 6

INGREDIENTS

- 2.1b. Beef round, sliced

- 2 tablespoons olive oil

- 2 garlic cloves, crushed

- 1 teaspoon salt

- 1 tablespoon dijon mustard

- 1 cup balsamic vinegar

INSTRUCTIONS

1. Fill a plastic bag with the steak and seal it.

2. In a bowl, mix the remaining ingredients.

3   Mix well.

4   Fill the plastic bag with the mixture.

5   Place for 12 hours in the refrigerator.

6   Eliminate the marinade.

7   To the food dehydrator, add the beef slices and dehydrate at 165°F for 6hours.

NUTRIENTS:

Kcal: 370, Fats: 27 g, Total Carbs: 9 g, Proteins: 23 g.

Buffalo Jerky In A Dehydrator

Prep Time: 15 hours

Dehydration Time: 6 hours | Servings: 4-6

INGREDIENTS

- 1 lb. Beef round, sliced

- 1 cup buffalo sauce

- 1 teaspoon salt

INSTRUCTIONS

1. Salt the meat slices.

2. Fill a bowl with the buffalo sauce and add the seasoned beef and stir.

3. Cover the bowl and put for 15 hours in the refrigerator.

4. Eliminate the marinade.

5. Dehydrate the beef for 6 hours at 165°F.

NUTRIENTS:

Kcal: 370, Fats: 24 g, Total Carbs: 2.5 g, Proteins: 21 g.

☆ ☆ ☆ ☆ ☆

Sweet and Sour Pork

Prep Time: 12 hours | Cook Time: 0 minutes

Dehydration Time: 6 hours | Servings: 6

INGREDIENTS

- 1 lb. Pork tenderloin, sliced

- 1 shallot, grated

- 2 garlic cloves, grated

- 1/4 cup brown sugar

- 2 tablespoons fish sauce

- 1/4 cup lime juice

- Salt and pepper to taste

INSTRUCTIONS

1   In a bowl, combine all the ingredients and mix well.

2   Place in a plastic bag that can be sealed.

3   Put in the refrigerator for 12 hours.

4   Take out of the marinade and place the slices of pork in the fooddehydrator.

5   Process for 6 hours at 158 °F.

NUTRIENTS:

Kcal: 332, Fats: 29.4 g, Total Carbs: 9.3 g, Proteins: 25 g.

☆ ☆ ☆ ☆ ☆

Dehydrated Lamb Jerky

Prep Time: 12 hours

Dehydration Time: 6 hours | Servings: 4

INGREDIENTS

- 1 teaspoon garlic powder
- 3 lb. Leg of lamb, sliced
- 1/2 teaspoons onion powder
- 4 tablespoons Worcestershire sauce
- 1 tablespoon oregano
- 1/4 cup soy sauce
- Pepper to taste

INSTRUCTIONS

1. In a sealable plastic bag add the lamb slices.
2. Put the remaining ingredients in a bowl and mix well.
3. Pour the mixture into the sealable plastic bag and marinate in therefrigerator for 12 hours.
4. Place the lamb slices to the food dehydrator and process at 145°F for 6hours.

NUTRIENTS:

Kcal: 167, Fats: 5.1 g, Total Carbs: 27 g, Proteins: 689 g.

☆ ☆ ☆ ☆ ☆

Dehydrated Lemon Fish Jerky

Prep Time: 4 hours | Cook Time: 0 minutes

Dehydration Time: 8 hours | Servings: 2

INGREDIENTS

- 1 lb. Cod fillet, sliced

- 1 teaspoon lemon zest

- 2 tablespoons olive oil

- 1/2 tablespoon lemon juice

- 1 teaspoon dill

- Salt to taste

- 1 clove garlic, grated

INSTRUCTIONS

1   In a sealable plastic bag, put all the ingredients.

2   Put the plastic bag inside the refrigerator for 4 hours.

3   Then drain the marinade and add the fish slices to the food dehydrator.

4   Process at 145°F for 8 hours.

NUTRIENTS:

Kcal: 170, Fats: 26.8 g, Total Carbs: 7.9 g, Proteins: 7.2 g.

Cajun Fish Jerky

Prep Time: 4 hours | Cook Time: 0 minutes

Dehydration Time: 8 hours | Servings: 2-4

INGREDIENTS

- Salt and pepper to taste

- 1 1b. Cod fillet, sliced

- 1 teaspoon onion powder

- 1/4 teaspoon cayenne pepper

- 1 teaspoon garlic powder

- 1 teaspoon paprika

- 1 tablespoon lemon juice

INSTRUCTIONS

1 In a bowl mix the spices with lemon juice, salt and pepper.

2 Season the fish with this mixture and transfer all in a sealable plasticbag.

3 Put in the refrigerator for 4 hours.

4 Drain the marinade and arrange the salmon slices on the food dehydrator.

5 Dehydrate at 145°F for 8 hours.

NUTRIENTS:

Kcal: 391, Fats: 6.1 g, Total Carbs: 23 g, Proteins: 48.1 g.

☆ ☆ ☆ ☆ ☆

Chapter 7
Fruit Recipes

Watermelon Rind

Prep Time: 20 minutes | Cook Time: 10 minutes

Dehydration Time: 6 hours | Servings: 12

INGREDIENTS

- 4 cups of water

- 4 cups of white sugar

- 1 tbsp of dried basil

- 1/2 cup of spearmint leaves

- 1 watermelon rind

INSTRUCTIONS

1   You should cut the rind of the watermelon into pieces that are 2 inches long, 1 inch broad, and 1/2 inch thick.

2   Mix the water, basil, spearmint, and sugar in a large saucepan. Bring toa boil over high heat. You should strain both the spearmint and thebasil.

3   Add the watermelon's rind, ensuring that each piece is well submerged. About five minutes into the cooking process, the rind should be tender.

4   After the watermelon slices have been drained, place them in a single line on the dehydrator's trays.

5   Dry until the pieces are dried, between 6 and 8 hours.

NUTRIENTS:

Kcal: 381, Fats: 1.7 g, Total Carbs: 94.1 g, Proteins: 2.5 g.

Dehydrated Strawberries

Prep Time: 10 minutes | Cook Time: 15 minutes

Dehydration Time: 10 hours | Servings: 5

INGREDIENTS

- 1 pound of strawberries

1   **INSTRUCTIONS**

2   Wash and dry your strawberries. You can either pull them or cut off the green tips.

3   Cut the berries into slices that are about 1/8 of an inch thick. Make an effort to get the slices as even as you can so that they will dry in the same amount of time.

4   Place the strawberry slices on the dehydrator's trays, taking care that they do not come into contact with one another. This improves the passage of air and enables them to dry perfectly.

5   The dehydrator temperature should be set to 135°F, and the drying process should take between 6-10 hours. When you break them apart, they shouldn't be wet and have a very dry, almost brittle feel.

NUTRIENTS:

Kcal: 60, Fats: 1 g, Total Carbs: 25 g, Proteins: 1 g.

☆ ☆ ☆ ☆ ☆

Peanut Butter Fruit Roll

Prep Time: 5 minutes | Cook Time: 30 minutes

Dehydration Time: 4 hours | Servings: 2

INGREDIENTS

- 1 tbsp of peanut butter

- 2 bananas

INSTRUCTIONS

1 Peanut butter and bananas are blended at high speed for less than oneminute until a smooth consistency is reached.

2 A uniform layer should be created on the dehydrator sheet.

3 Dehydrate yourself for four to five hours at 125-135°F.

4 This dish is also successful when cooked in an oven: Make sure you usea baking sheet covered in parchment paper. 4-5 hours with the heat setto the lowest possible setting and the oven door slightly ajar.

NUTRIENTS:

Kcal: 207, Fats: 8 g, Total Carbs: 38 g, Proteins: 5 g.

Dried Apple Rings With Chips

Prep Time: 10 minutes | Cook Time: 5 minutes

Dehydration Time: 10 hours | Servings: 5-6

INGREDIENTS

- 1/2 cinnamon sticks

- 2 tbsp of lemon juice

- 2 pounds of apples

INSTRUCTIONS

1   Begin by selecting apples that you are familiar with and enjoy eating, ensuring they are not damaged.

2   If you wish to remove the wax from the apples, you may peel them or use a small amount of apple cider vinegar as a scrub.

3   Remove the core from the apple, and cut it into quarter-inch slices. For this purpose, the apple peeler can also be used for pears.

4   If you want to avoid the apples from becoming brown, you can keep them from browning by dipping them in water with lemon juice.

5   The apples will turn brown if you don't dehydrate them, but they will still taste excellent and are completely safe to consume.

6   On the dehydrator's trays, place the apples in a single layer; if you choose, you can sprinkle them with a cinnamon sugar mixture at this point.

7   Apples need roughly 10 hours of dehydration time at 135°F. You can even dehydrate them in the oven, provided that your oven can reach thatlow temperature.

8   When the apple ring slices have the texture of leather but have lost theircrispiness, they are ready to be eaten. If you prefer dried apple rings thatare more similar to apple chips after they have been dehydrated, keep them in the dehydrator for longer.

9   Apples that have been dried can be kept for up to half a year in anairtight container.

NUTRIENTS:

Kcal: 107, Fats: 8 g, Total Carbs: 48 g, Proteins: 5 g.

☆ ☆ ☆ ☆ ☆

Dehydrated Fig Balls

Prep Time: 12 minutes | Cook Time: 0 minutes

Dehydration Time: 6 hours | Servings: 6

INGREDIENTS

- 12 dried figs
- 3/4 cup unsweetened coconut flakes
- 1 cup raw almonds
- 1/2 cup raisins
- 1 tsp. Almond extract
- 1 tsp. Vanilla extract

INSTRUCTIONS

1. In a food processor put all the ingredients and pulse until they areground.

2. When the mixture has a dough-like consistency, roll into balls. Roll the balls in the coconut flakes and place it on dehydrator trays.

3. Dehydrate for 6 hours at 135°F.

NUTRIENTS:

Kcal: 150, Fats: 9.4 g, Total Carbs: 15 g, Proteins: 2.1 g.

☆ ☆ ☆ ☆ ☆

Dehydrated Blackberries

Prep Time: 15 minutes | Cook Time: 0 minutes

Dehydration Time: 2-3 hours | Servings: 6

INGREDIENTS

- 1 lb. Blackberries

- 1/2 tablespoons white sugar

INSTRUCTIONS

1   In a blender put the blackberries and sugar.

2   Pulse and strain the mixture to remove the seeds.

3   Pour the fruit liquid into a fruit roll sheet and place these in the fooddehydrator.

4   Dehydrate for 3 hours at 165°F.

NUTRIENTS:

Kcal: 433, Fats: 5.4 g, Total Carbs: 108 g, Proteins: 0 g.

★ ★ ★ ★ ☆

Dehydrated Apricots With Vanilla

Prep Time: 15 minutes | Cook Time: 0 minutes

Dehydration Time: 9-10 hours | Servings: 4

INGREDIENTS

- 10 medium sized apricots, pitted

- 4 tbsp. Warm water

- 1 1/2 tsp. Honey

- Seeds from one vanilla bean, scraped out

INSTRUCTIONS

1   In a bowl, add water with honey and vanilla seeds and stir to combine. Combine vanilla seeds are well separated.

2   Slice the apricots into thin slices and place them on the dehydrator tray and brush with a thin layer of vanilla mixture. It is not required that all vanilla seeds adhere to the fruit.

3   Dehydrate for 9-10 hours at 135°F.

NUTRIENTS:

Kcal: 323, Fats: 0.3 g, Total Carbs: 57 g, Proteins: 4.2 g.

Honey Bourbon Peaches

Prep Time: 4 hours | Cook Time: 0 minutes

Dehydration Time: 16 hours | Servings: 1

INGREDIENTS

- 3 tablespoons bourbon

- 1 peach, cored and sliced

- 1/4 cup hot water

- 1/4 cup honey

INSTRUCTIONS

1.   In a sealable plastic bag, place the slices.

2.   In a bowl, mix the hot water with honey, until has been dissolved.

3.   Add the bourbon and let cool.

4.   Once cool, add the marinade to the plastic bag and marinate

for 4 hours.

5. Drain the marinade and add these to the food dehydrator.

6. Dehydrate for 16 hours at 145°F.

NUTRIENTS:

Kcal: 381, Fats: 6.8 g, Total Carbs: 22 g, Proteins: 48.2 g.

Dehydrated Raspberry Rolls

Prep Time: 15 minutes | Cook Time: 0 minutes

Dehydration Time: 5 hours | Servings: 6

INGREDIENTS

- 1 lb. Raspberries

- 2 1/2 tablespoons sugar

INSTRUCTIONS

1. In a blender, add the raspberries and sugar and blend until smooth.

2. Strain to remove the seeds.

3. Add the liquid to a fruit roll sheet and place this in the food dehydrator.

4. Dehydrate for 5 hours at 165°F.

NUTRIENTS:

Kcal: 391, Fats: 6.1 g, Total Carbs: 23 g, Proteins: 51 g.

Orange Fruit Leather

Prep Time: 12 minutes | Cook Time: 0 minutes

Dehydration Time: 6 hours | Servings: 4

INGREDIENTS

- 1 cup applesauce

- 4 cups Vanilla yogurt

- 1 cup orange juice concentrate

INSTRUCTIONS

1. In a blender, pulse all the ingredients, until smooth.

2. Spread the mixture onto the roll sheet and place this in the fooddehydrator.

3. Dry at 135°F for 6 hours.

NUTRIENTS:

Kcal: 160, Fats: 11.4 g, Total Carbs: 6.5 g, Proteins: 6.1 g.

☆ ☆ ☆ ☆ ☆

Dehydrated Lemon Slices

Prep Time: 3 minutes | Cook Time: 0 minutes

Dehydration Time: 6 hours | Servings: 2

INGREDIENTS

- 2 lemons, sliced

INSTRUCTIONS

1. Arrange the lemon slices in the food dehydrator.

2. Dry the lemon for 6 hours at 125°F.

NUTRIENTS:

Kcal: 132, Fats: 0 g, Total Carbs: 31 g, Proteins: 0g.

☆ ☆ ☆ ☆ ☆

Berry Fruit Leather

Prep Time: 8 minutes | Cook Time: 0 minutes

Dehydration Time: 6 hours | Servings: 4

INGREDIENTS

- 1 teaspoon vanilla extract

- 1 lb. Strawberries

- 1/2 cup raspberries

INSTRUCTIONS

1   Put all the ingredients in a blender and pulse until smooth.

2   Strain to remove seeds.

3   Pour the fruit puree into a fruit roll sheet and place in the fooddehydrator.

4   Dehydrate for 6 hours at 165°F.

NUTRIENTS:

Kcal: 37, Fats: 0 g, Total Carbs: 7.9 g, Proteins: 0.2 g.

☆ ☆ ☆ ☆ ☆

Dried Cranberries Sweet and Sour

Prep Time: 13 minutes | Cook Time: 0 minutes

Dehydration Time: 12 hours | Servings: 6

INGREDIENTS

- 1 1/2 cups of Cranberries
- 1/4 cup corn syrup (or sugar)
- 1 orange zest
- 1 lime zest

INSTRUCTIONS

1. In a bowl, pour boiling water over cranberries them until the skinscrack. Drain the cranberries and mix them with the rest of the ingredients.

2. Place berries on cooking sheet and freeze for 2 hours to promote faster drying.

3. Spread the berries onto the mesh sheet and place this in the fooddehydrator

4. Dry at 135°F for 12 hours.

NUTRIENTS:

Kcal: 46, Fats: 0.2 g, Total Carbs: 10 g, Proteins: 0.2 g.

Pineapple Chips

Prep Time: 13 minutes | Cook Time: 0 minutes

Dehydration Time: 12 hours | Servings: 4-6

INGREDIENTS

- 1 pineapple peeled and cored

- Sea salt to taste

- 1/2 cup sweetened coconut flakes

- Coconut oil

INSTRUCTIONS

1. Slice pineapple into thin, uniform rounds about 1/2 inch thick.

2. On each pineapple slice, spread a thin layer of coconut oil and sprinklewith a small amount of salt and coconut flakes.

3. Arrange in your dehydrator and dry for 12 hours to 135°F.

4. Flipping the slices halfway through for even drying.

NUTRIENTS:

Kcal: 55, Fats: 2.1 g, Total Carbs: 6.3 g, Proteins: 1 g.

Chapter 8
Herbs & Powders

Veggie Stock Powder

Prep Time: 20 minutes | Cook Time: 15 minutes

Dehydration Time: 10 hours | Servings: 4

INGREDIENTS

- 1 tbsp of salt

- 6 ribs

- 8 garlic cloves

- 2 onions

- 1 large leek

- 8-10 mushrooms

- 2 large carrots

INSTRUCTIONS

1   After being washed and peeled, the vegetables should be sliced intobite-sized pieces.

2   Arrange the vegetables in a pattern on the trays of the dehydrator thathave been lined with silicon mesh. Check out the advice up top.

3   The temperature should be set at 75°C, and the timer should be on for 8-10 hours.

4   Once your vegetables have been dried, set them aside on the trays tocool and let them acclimate to room temperature for 1-2 hours.

5   Place the dehydrated veggies in a big bowl or immediately into thecontainer that comes with the Vibe blender.

6   To taste, add the salt.

7   To activate the 'pulse' function, press the button many times.

8   Remove the jug from its base, then give it a good shake with your freehand.

9   Place the jug back on the counter and process the dried vegetables untilthey become a powder.

10 Place the powdered vegetables in a jar made of glass and cover it withthe lid.

11 Keep it in the pantry, away from dampness and direct sunshine, andconsume it within three months at the most.

NUTRIENTS:

Kcal: 87, Fats: 0 g, Total Carbs: 57 g, Proteins: 0 g.

☆ ☆ ☆ ☆ ☆

Herb Mix

Prep Time: 15 minutes | Cook Time: 30 minutes

Dehydration Time: 6 hours | Servings: 18

INGREDIENTS

- 1 medium lemons

- 1 tbsp of sea salt

- 1/2 cup of oregano

- 3/4 cup of thyme

- 3 tbsp of garlic flakes

- 1/4 cup of rosemary

INSTRUCTIONS

1   Put an oven rack in the center and preheat at 170°F.

2   You should spread the herbs and the lemon zest on a cookie sheet, thenput the sheet in the center of the oven.

3   Allow the herbs to dry in the oven for two to four hours, turning themixture over once every half an hour or so.

4   Take the pan out of the oven when the herb mixture reaches the pointwhere it feels dry. Please allow the herbs to cool.

5   After it has had time to dry and cool down, you should transfer themixture to a bowl.

6   Crush the herbs between your fingers, add garlic and salt to the mixture,and stir.

7   Place the mixture in a jar or other container to keep out air.

NUTRIENTS:

Kcal: 11, Fats: 1 g, Total Carbs: 3 g, Proteins: 1 g.

☆ ☆ ☆ ☆ ☆

Dried Powdered Basil

Prep Time: 10 minutes | Cook Time: 30 minutes

Dehydration Time: 12 hours | Servings: 4

INGREDIENTS

- 1 blender

- 1 airtight container

- 3 cups of fresh basil

- 1 dehydrator

INSTRUCTIONS

1   Gather your fresh basil, give the leaves a quick rinse, and then

spread them out on the mesh trays of a dehydrator. I ended up using all three ofthe trays. Anything less than three trays will probably not blend well enough; it is essential to have sufficient basil for the blender to function correctly.

2   Dehydrate for 10–15 hours at 105°F. I provide a range because the amount of time required to dehydrate food varies depending on the machine used and the location of the kitchen.

3   After the basil has lost all its moisture, put it in a powerful blender like aVitamix and puree it until smooth.

4   To a greater extent that you have basil, the blender can process it more effectively. You could try grinding the beans in a food processor or a coffee grinder, although I haven't personally used any of those tools.

5   Place in a spice jar and use it in any basil dish that strikes your fancy.

NUTRIENTS:

Kcal: 7, Fats: 0 g, Total Carbs: 3 g, Proteins: 1 g.

☆ ☆ ☆ ☆ ☆

Garlic Powder

Prep Time: 15 minutes | Cook Time: 1 hour

Dehydrating Time: 12 hours | Servings: 24

INGREDIENTS

- 6 heads garlic

INSTRUCTIONS

1   Take the head of the garlic and separate the cloves from it. To prepare the cloves, remove their papery skins and slice

them very thinly.

2. Dehydrator instructions for drying garlic are as follows: Dehydrate the sliced garlic at 125°F for up to 12 hours.

3. Arrange the garlic out in a single layer on the dehydrator screens.Repeatedly rotating your screens will ensure that they dry evenly.

4. To dry garlic in an oven, dry the sliced garlic in an oven preheated to 150–200°F for 1-2 hours, or until the garlic snaps when it is broken. Spread the garlic out on a baking sheet lined with parchment paper.

5. After allowing the dehydrated garlic to reach room temperature, place itin a powerful blender, spice grinder, or coffee grinder and process it until it becomes a powder.

6. Sift the powder to remove any large pieces, then store it in an airtight container in a dark, cool, and dry location. You should keep garlic powder at room temperature.

7. You can make approximately half a cup of garlic powder from six large heads of garlic. For every clove of garlic in a recipe, substitute 1/8 teaspoon of garlic powder.

NUTRIENTS:

Kcal: 9, Fats: 0 g, Total Carbs: 2 g, Proteins: 0.5 g.

☆ ☆ ☆ ☆ ☆

Dehydrated Red Lentil Chili

Prep Time: 15 minutes | Cook Time: 30 minutes

Dehydrating time: 10 hours | Servings: 4

INGREDIENTS

- 1 tsp of salt

- 1 tsp of sugar

- 1 tbsp of ground cumin

- 3 tbsp of chili powder

- 2 tbsp of tomato paste

- 6 cloves garlic

- 1 tbsp of oil

- 2 cups of vegetable broth

- 1 cup of diced onion

- 1 can of roasted tomatoes

- 1 cup of diced bell pepper

- 2 cups of zucchini

- 1 can of kidney beans

- 1 cup of red lentils

INSTRUCTIONS

1   In a large container or Dutch oven, bring the oil to a temperature of medium heat. As the oil becomes hot, add the onions, peppers, and salt, and then sauté the mixture until the onions and peppers become softer.

2   Cook the vegetables until they turn golden in a few spots, then add the zucchini. Sauté the garlic, cumin, and chili powder until their aromas become predominant.

3   After adding the tomatoes, beans, and tomato paste to the two cups of broth, whisk to blend the ingredients. After bringing to a simmer, add the lentils to the pot.

4   Simmer for twenty minutes, giving the lentils the occasional stir until they reach the desired tenderness; if necessary, add more water. You should then mix in sugar and adjust the

seasoning to taste. Take the pan off the heat.

5   To dry the chili, spread it out in a uniform layer on dehydrator trays lined with sheets of solid fruit leather, and make sure the layer is as thin as possible.

6   Dehydrate the chili at 135°F for 8-12 hours, or until it is dry andcrumbly.

7   If you want to keep them for a longer period, you should package them in bags that can be sealed and keep them in a cool, dark area or the freezer.

8   Put the chile that has been dehydrated and a bottle of olive oil withabout three to four tablespoons total in your barrel.

9   Place the chili, approximately one cup of water for each serving, andone tablespoon of oil per serving in a cookpot at the time of the meal.

10 Bring to a boil, immediately reduce the heat to a simmer and continue cooking for approximately ten minutes while stirring often, or until the beans and lentils are cooked.

NUTRIENTS:

Kcal: 520, Fats: 19 g, Total Carbs: 66 g, Proteins: 22 g.

Onion Powder

Prep Time: 12 minutes | Cook Time: 0 minutes

Dehydration Time: 8 hours | Servings: 4

INGREDIENTS

- 5 onions, sliced

INSTRUCTIONS

1. Arrange the onion slices in a single layer in the food dehydrator anddehydrate for 8 hours at 145°F.

2. Transfer the dried onion to a food processor and pulse until powdered.

NUTRIENTS:

Kcal: 87, Fats: 0 g, Total Carbs: 5.1 g, Proteins: 3.1 g.

Tomato Powder

Prep Time: 13 minutes | Cook Time: 0 minutes

Dehydration Time: 12 hours | Servings: 6

INGREDIENTS

- Skin of 12 tomatoes

INSTRUCTIONS

1. In a food dehydrator place the tomato skins.

2. Dry for 12 hours at 135°F

3. Transfer the dried tomatoes in a blender and pulse until the mixtureturns to powder.

NUTRIENTS:

Kcal: 24, Fats: 0 g, Total Carbs: 2.3 g, Proteins: 1.3 g.

Basil, Oregano and Parsley Powder

Prep Time: 10 minutes | Cook Time: 0 minutes

Dehydration Time: 8 hours | Servings: 4

INGREDIENTS

- 2 tablespoons basil leaves
- 2 tablespoons oregano leaves
- 2 tablespoons parsley leaves
- 2 tablespoons salt
- 2 tablespoons brown sugar

INSTRUCTIONS

1. Into the food dehydrator, place the herb leaves.

2. Dehydrate for 8 hours at 135°F

3. Transfer the dried leaves in a blender and pulse until the mixture turnsto powder.

4. Stir with the sugar and salt.

NUTRIENTS:

Kcal: 97, Fats: 1 g, Total Carbs:11 g, Proteins: 7.1 g.

Kimchi Powder

Prep Time: 3 minutes | Cook Time: 0 minutes

Dehydrating Time: 12 hours | Servings: 4

INGREDIENTS

- 2 cups kimchi

INSTRUCTIONS

1 Into the food dehydrator, place the kimchi.

2 Dehydrate for 12 hours at 155°F

3 Transfer the kimchi in a blender and pulse until the mixture turns topowder.

NUTRIENTS:

Kcal: 79, Fats: 4 g, Total Carbs: 4 g, Proteins: 3.5 g.

Chapter 9
Nuts & Seeds

Dehydrated Banana-Pecan Cake

Prep Time: 20 minutes | Cook Time: 30 minutes

Dehydration Time: 8 hours | Servings: 6-8

INGREDIENTS

- 1 lemon

- 2 cups of sugar

- 1 1/2 tbsp of baking powder

- 11/2 cup of softened butter

- 4 eggs

- 1/2 pounds of pecan pieces

- 3 cups of flour

- 4 bananas

INSTRUCTIONS

1. You should mix eggs, butter, and sugar in a large bowl.

2. Mash bananas. After cleaning the lemon, grate the peel over the bananasto add flavor. After that, pour the entirety of the lemon juice over the bananas. To the bowl, please add.

3. Toss all ingredients in a bowl until everything is thoroughly incorporated.

4. After lining a loaf pan with baking paper measuring 12 inches in length,pour the batter into the pan.

5. 75–80 minutes at 350°F in an oven that has been warmed and set to the fan setting. During the first 70 minutes, you should not open the oven door at all.

6. Slice the bread into pieces that are approximately 1/8 of an inch thick. After that, split each slice into three equal parts.

7   Dehydrate for around 5 hours at 125°F. When done, the dehydratedcake will have the crunchiness of cookies and will be very easy to breakin two.

8   These cake-cookie hybrid dehydrated treats are perfect for munching onwhile hiking, and you can also crumble them up and add them torehydrated fruit or oatmeal.

NUTRIENTS:

Kcal: 50, Fats: 2.4 g, Total Carbs: 15.8 g, Proteins: 3.9 g.

Dehydrator Cookies

Prep Time: 20 minutes | Cook Time: 30 minutes

Dehydrating Time: 16 hours | Servings: 4

INGREDIENTS

- 1/4 tsp of ground cinnamon

- 1/4 cup of honey

- 1/4 tsp of ground cardamom

- 1/4 tsp of ground cloves

- 1 cup of pumpkin puree

- 3/4 tsp of ground nutmeg

- 3/4 tsp of ground ginger

- 3/4 tsp of ground allspice

- 1/2 cup of coconut cream concentrate

INSTRUCTIONS

1   In a bowl, properly combine all of the ingredients.

2   Prepare your food dehydrator by inserting the fruit roll sheets.

3   Place approximately 2 tablespoons of batter per cookie on each of your Fruit Roll Sheets using heaping dessert spoons.

4   Mold the blobs of batter into cookies by spreading them out with the back of a spoon until they have a diameter of about 2 inches and aheight of about 1/2 inch.

5   Allow cookies to air dry for 12 to 16 hours, or until the exterior is slightly crisp and the interior is cakey or dry longer for a crisper cookie.

6   After 10 to 12 hours, I like to remove the cookies from the fruit roll sheet and place them on the dehydrator tray. This helps ensure that the bottom of each cookie dries out evenly.

NUTRIENTS:

Kcal: 59, Fats: 0.8 g, Total Carbs: 11 g, Proteins: 2.2 g.

☆ ☆ ☆ ☆ ☆

Bagel Flax Crackers

Prep Time: 5 minutes | Cook Time: 0 minutes

Dehydrating Time: 24 hours | Servings: 24

INGREDIENTS

- 3 tsp of sea salt

- 3 tsp of onion flakes

- 3 tsp of garlic flakes

- 3 tsp of sesame seeds

- 3 tsp of poppy seeds

- 1 clove garlic

- 1 1/2 cups of water

- 3/4 cup of golden flax seeds

- 1/4 cup of brown flax seeds

INSTRUCTIONS

1   Combine the water and garlic in a food processor, blender, or Nutribullet. Pour over flax seeds. Soak for around three and a halfhours. The mixture will eventually turn gelatinous.

2   Spread the mixture onto a Teflon sheet to a thickness of 1/8 and ¼ inch.Make squares out of the mix using a knife to cut lines into the crackers to create grids.

3   Combine the spices in a bowl, excluding the table salt. It would be best if you sprinkled everything mixed on top of the crackers. After that, sprinkle some coarse sea salt on top.

4   Dehydrate at 110°F for 24 hours or until the food is crispy.

NUTRIENTS:

Kcal: 44, Fats: 0 g, Total Carbs: 3 g, Proteins: 1 g.

☆ ☆ ☆ ☆ ☆

Graham Crackers

Prep Time: 10 minutes | Cook Time: 20

minutes Dehydration Time: 6 hours | Servings:

8 INGREDIENTS

- 1/2 tsp of cinnamon

- 1 cup of ground peanuts

- 2 1/2 cup of creamy peanut butter

- 3 bananas

- 1/2 cups of graham cracker crumbs

INSTRUCTIONS

1 You should mash bananas in a big bowl and then fold peanut butter.

2 It would help if you mixed cinnamon, peanuts, and graham cracker crumbs until they are completely incorporated.

3 Create a ball out of the dough.

4 Position on a big sheet of waxed paper and form into a long rectanglebefore setting it aside.

5 You should wrap wax paper securely around the dough, then chill it forfour to six hours or overnight.

6 Use a knife with an edge to cut the dough into quarter-inch slices.

7 Position on standard baking sheets and dry at 145°F for 4-6 hours, oruntil firm.

NUTRIENTS:

Kcal: 349, Fats: 19.9 g, Total Carbs: 36.5 g, Proteins: 11.1g.

☆ ☆ ☆ ☆ ☆

Almond Cranberry Cookies

Prep Time: 12 minutes | Cook Time: 0 minutes

Dehydration Time: 6 hours | Servings: 4-6

INGREDIENTS

- 1 banana

- 1 tbsp. Honey

- Wet pulp from almond milk

- 2 tbsp. Coconut oil

- 1/2 cup almonds, coarsely chopped

- 3/4 cup shredded coconut flakes

- 1/2 cup dried cranberries

INSTRUCTIONS

1   In a food processor, mix all the ingredients. Place a small scoop of dough on dehydrator sheets and flatten into a cookie.

2   Dehydrate for 6 hours at 105°F.

NUTRIENTS:

Kcal: 90, Fats: 7.4 g, Total Carbs: 5.8 g, Proteins: 2.9 g.

☆ ☆ ☆ ☆ ☆

Fruit and Nut Balls

Prep Time: 13 minutes | Cook Time: 0 minutes

Dehydrating Time: 6 hours | Servings: 6

INGREDIENTS

- 1 cup dried dates

- 1 cup dried apricots

- 1 cup dried cranberries

- 1 cup flaked coconut

- 1 cup crushed pecans

- 1 cup figs

- 1 cup dried cherries

- 1 cup crushed almonds

- 3 tsp. Coconut oil, melted

INSTRUCTIONS

1. In a food processor pulse figs, cherries, dates, apricots and cranberries.

2. In a bowl add the mixture and mix with nuts and coconut oil.

3. Shape into 1" balls and roll balls in coconut.

4. Place in food dehydrator and dry for 6 hours at 135°F.

NUTRIENTS:

Kcal: 100, Fats: 8 g, Total Carbs: 7 g, Proteins: 2.1 g.

Fruits and Nuts Clusters

Prep Time: 13 minutes | Cook Time: 0 minutes

Dehydration Time: 6 hours | Servings: 5

INGREDIENTS

- 10 dates, pitted

- 1 tsp. Salt

- 1 tsp. Vanilla extract

- 2 cups cashews

- 1 cup dried blueberries

- 1 cup rolled oats, raw

- 1/2 cup cashew butter

- 1/2 cup maple syrup

- 1 1/2 tsp. Cinnamon

- 1 cup pecans

- 1 cup dried cranberries

INSTRUCTIONS

1   In a food processor, pulse until smooth, maple syrup, cinnamon, vanillaextract, cashew butter, salt and dates.

2   In a bowl, mix cashews, dried fruits, pecans and oats. Pour liquidmixture on top and toss to coat.

3   Pour batter onto dehydrator sheets and dehydrate for 1 hour at 145°F.

4   Reduce temperature to 115°F and continue dehydrating for 5 hours

NUTRIENTS:

Kcal: 112, Fats: 8 g, Total Carbs: 9 g, Proteins: 3.1 g.

☆ ☆ ☆ ☆ ☆

Lemon-Hazelnut Crackers

Prep Time: 13 minutes | Cook Time: 0 minutes

Dehydration Time: 8 hours | Servings: 6

INGREDIENTS

- 1 cup chia seeds

- 1 cup water

- 1 1/2 tbsp. Lemon zest

- 1 tbsp. Maple syrup

- 4 cups hazelnuts, soaked overnight, skins removed

- 1 tsp. Sea salt

- Black pepper to taste

INSTRUCTIONS

1   In 1 cup water, mix chia seeds and allow to soften.

2   In food processor blend the hazelnuts until fine.

3   In a bowl, pour ground nuts with chia seeds, maple syrup, lemon zest,salt and pepper.

4   Spread onto dehydrator trays and dehydrate for 1 hour at 145°F.Decrease heat to 115°F and continue to dehydrate for 7 hours.

NUTRIENTS:

Kcal: 159, Fats: 15.4 g, Total Carbs: 5.8 g, Proteins: 4.9 g.

Macadamia-Sage Crackers

Prep Time: 13 minutes | Cook Time: 0 minutes

Dehydrating Time: 12 hours | Servings: 4

INGREDIENTS

- 2 cups macadamia nuts

- 3 cups water

- 1/2 cup olive oil

- 2 cups chia or flax seeds

- 1 1/2 tbsp. Fresh sage, crushed

- Sea salt and white pepper to taste

INSTRUCTIONS

1 In a food processor blend macadamia nuts, flax seeds, sage, salt andpepper. Process until you have a fine texture.

2 In a bowl, add the water a little at a time to the seed and nut mix and stiruntil thick.

3 Spread the dough on dehydrator sheets and season with olive oil and seasalt.

4 Dehydrate at 110°F for 4 hours. Score the crackers, flip them over anddehydrate another 8 hours.

NUTRIENTS:

Kcal: 179, Fats: 15.8 g, Total Carbs: 71 g, Proteins: 7 g.

Pepita Onion Crackers

Prep Time: 13 minutes | Cook Time: 0 minutes

Dehydrating Time: 8 hours | Servings: 4

INGREDIENTS

- 1/2 cup pepitas

- 1 cups sprouted quinoa

- 2 cloves garlic

- 3/4 cup chia seeds, finely ground

- 1/4 cup low sodium soy sauce

- 1 tsp. Onion powder

- 1/2 tsp. Salt

INSTRUCTIONS

1   In a food processor blend all the other ingredients except pepitas andpulse until well combined.

2   Spread mixture on dehydrator sheets and sprinkle pepitas on top andpress down to adhere to mixture.

3   Cut into squares and dehydrate for 8 hours at 140°F

NUTRIENTS:

Kcal: 104, Fats: 4 g, Total Carbs: 15 g, Proteins: 4 g.

☆ ☆ ☆ ☆ ☆

Raw Granola

Prep Time: 10 minutes | Cook Time: 0 minutes

Dehydration Time: 14 hours | Servings: 6

INGREDIENTS

- 4 cups rolled oats

- 1/4 cup oat bran

- 1 1/2 cup walnuts, pecans or almonds

- 1 cup honey

- 1 cup coconut oil, melted

- 1 1/2 cup raw sunflower seeds

- 1 1/2 cup raw pumpkin seeds

- 1 1/2 cup coconut

- 1 cup water

- 1 tsp. Cinnamon

- 1/2 tsp. Nutmeg

INSTRUCTIONS

1. In a bowl mix together all the ingredients. Add all the spread mixtureonto dehydrator sheets

2. Dehydrate for 14 hours at 115°F.

NUTRIENTS:

Kcal: 130, Fats: 8 g, Total Carbs: 12 g, Proteins: 5 g.

☆ ☆ ☆ ☆ ☆

Seasoned Sunflower Seeds

Prep Time: 13 minutes | Cook Time: 0 minutes

Dehydration Time: 16 hours | Servings: 6

INGREDIENTS

- 3 cups shelled sunflower seeds, raw

- 2 tbsp. Olive oil

- 1 tsp. Onion powder

- 1 tsp. Celery salt

- 1 tbsp. Soy sauce

- 1 tsp. Garlic powder

- 1/2 tsp. Crushed red pepper flakes

INSTRUCTIONS

1. In a bowl, soak sunflower seeds overnight. Rinse and dry.

2. Mix together the seeds with all the remaining ingredients.

3. Place on a dehydrator tray and dehydrate at 115°F for 16 hours.

NUTRIENTS:

Kcal: 150, Fats: 12.4 g, Total Carbs: 5.8 g, Proteins: 4.9 g.

Conclusion

Drying food is one of the oldest ways of food preservation that humans have discovered. Since ancient times, humans have preserved meat, fish, and food plants by drying them in the sun or the naturally dry air of deserts and mountains. This technique is still an essential part of the way of life in many rural communities. To save themselves from starving during the harsh winter months, Native Americans often utilized it to cure meat and preserve food reserves for later use.

Using this straightforward and efficient approach, you will be able to store food in a way that is not only efficient but also tasty, portable, and long- lasting. These are the characteristics that you want in precarious conditions. Not much equipment is required, and most of it is either already in your possession or can be acquired for a little cost. Dry meals have such low amounts of moisture that the organisms that cause food to go bad cannot existin them. This is the key to the success of dry foods.

As you know by now, drying is an excellent method for preserving your crop.Dried fruits and veggies are delicious, low in weight, simple to prepare, and jam-packed with various essential nutrients. There are several benefits to drying your own food, one of which is the significant reduction in the required storage space. For instance, you may keep 18 to 20 dried tomatoes ina jar or a bag that can be sealed back up again.

Drying food does not fully keep its consistency, flavor, look, or nutritional value as canning or freezing does. Hence some individuals think that drying food is not as good an option. On the other hand, dried foods are an excellent option for obtaining enough nourishment when on the road or when other meals are unavailable.

In a crisis, when fresh or frozen meals cannot be obtained, dried foods may be of great use. Dry meals are favored by many individuals who are concerned with disaster preparation because they need no refrigeration and take up very little space.

Drying at home may be accomplished in various ways; the dried substance primarily determines the approach used. Other procedures call for a dehydrator, while others need an oven. This book explains every method in detail. Many people prefer the sun for drying clothes, but for it to work, theair has to be extremely hot and dry. To a considerable extent, it is determined by factors such as geography, climate, and the kinds of equipment at one's disposal. This book also provides you with many easy recipes. Now that you have read the book, start prepping by making those foods.